# Healing the Purpose of Your Life

### Dennis Linn
### Sheila Fabricant Linn
### Matthew Linn, S.J.

ILLUSTRATIONS BY FRANCISCO MIRANDA

Paulist Press
New York/Mahwah, New Jersey

## Acknowledgments

We want to gratefully thank the following persons for their help and loving care in the preparation of this manuscript: Patricia Berne & Lou Savary, Jim & Mary Jo Brauner, Connor Cox, Marie Cox, Dolores Curran, Loic Fabricant, Walter Hanss, Paul & Sally Johnston, Mike Johnston, Barbara & Morton Kelsey, Jack McGinnis, Beatriz & Francisco Miranda, Judith Rock, Judy Ryan, Bob Sears, S.J.

Book Design by Saija Autrand, Faces Type & Design

IMPRIMI POTEST:
D. Edward Mathie, S.J.
*Provincial, Wisconsin Province of the Society of Jesus*
February 24, 1998

Library of Congress Cataloging-in-Publication Data

Linn, Dennis.
    Healing the purpose of your life / Dennis Linn, Sheila Fabricant Linn, Matthew Linn; illustrations by Francisco Miranda.
        p.   cm.
    Includes bibliographical references.
    ISBN 0-8091-3853-0
    1. Christian life—Catholic authors.   I. Linn, Sheila Fabricant.   II. Linn, Matthew.
III. Title.
    BX2350.2.L493   1999
    248.4′82—dc21                                                          98-46198
                                                                              CIP

Published by Paulist Press
997 Macarthur Boulevard
Mahwah, New Jersey 07430

www.paulistpress.com

Printed and bound in Mexico

# *Table of Contents*

*We dedicate this book to*
*John Matthew Linn.*
*We're so very glad you came.*

# *Song of the Spirit*

There is a tribe in East Africa in which . . . the birth date of a child is not counted from the day of its physical birth nor even the day of its conception, as in other village cultures. For this tribe the birth date comes the first time the child is a thought in its mother's mind. Aware of her intention to conceive a child with a particular father, the mother then goes off to sit alone under a tree. There she sits and listens until she can hear the song of the child that she hopes to conceive. Once she has heard it, she returns to her village and teaches it to the father so that

they can sing it together as they make love, inviting the child to join them. After the child is conceived, she sings it to the baby in her womb. Then she teaches it to the old women and midwives of her village, so that throughout the labor and at the miraculous moment of birth itself, the child is greeted with its song. After the birth, all the villagers learn the song of their new member and sing it to the child when it falls or hurts itself. It is sung in times of triumph, or in rituals and initiations. This song becomes a part of the marriage ceremony when the child is grown, and at the end of life, his or her loved ones will gather around the deathbed and sing this song for the last time.

Jack Kornfield

# *Introduction*

Our seven-year-old friend, Connor, came down for breakfast one morning and had the following conversation with his mother, Marie:

Connor: Mom, I have realized that I'm here for a very important purpose.

Marie: *(restraining her temptation to ask if he needed to go to the bathroom because they were leaving in five minutes)* Really? Do you want to tell me more about that?

Connor: Well, I know I'm here for some really important reason and I don't know what it is but it's gonna change the whole world. Everyone in the whole world is gonna know me because of this thing I'm gonna do.

Marie: *(by now hoping he'll keep talking)* Do you think it's something scientific or maybe in the art area?

*Connor:*  I have no idea what it is. All I know is it's really important and I
           have to do it and the world is gonna be better after I do it.
*Marie:*   Well, Connor, if there's ever anything we can do to help you, let
           us know.
*Connor:*  *(on his way back upstairs)* OK!

Like Connor, every one of us has a special reason for being here. One of our teachers was the great Episcopal mystic and healer, Agnes Sanford. Agnes called her autobiography *Sealed Orders,* to express her belief that each of us comes into this world with sealed orders from God. When we first heard that title, we felt some discomfort. It sounded militaristic and as if our life on earth was predestined in a way that precluded human freedom. However, when we read Agnes' book we realized that she called it *Sealed Orders* as a way of emphasizing the dignity and unique meaning of each person's life.

By "sealed orders," Agnes meant that it is as if before we were born each of us talked over with God our special purpose in this world. Rather than obeying commands in a militaristic sense, our sealed orders are something that we agreed to in the context of a loving dialogue with the God who created us. They are not first of all a task we are to complete, but rather our special way of being.

## Sealed Orders Are First of All a Way of Being

People who know the three of us might describe our sealed orders with words like "author," "priest," "healer," "retreat director," etc. These are all things that we *do*, and they are indeed part of our sealed orders as we understand them. However, our sealed orders are first of all a way of *being*. Herbert Alphonso, S.J., says that our "personal vocation" (his term for our special way of being) is "*the spirit* that animates" everything we do.

In Chapter 3 each of us will describe the spirit or special way of being that animates all our "doings." Sheila's special way of being is to care for the goodness in creation, Dennis' is to be a brother, and Matt's is to make things whole. The "doings" we have chosen (writing books, giving healing retreats, etc.) are part of our sealed orders only to the extent that they enhance or help us live out our special way of being. If we could never write another book or give another retreat, we would each still have a purpose in life because we would each still have our special way of being.

## Our Sealed Orders Are Our Essence

We believe our sealed orders are as much a part of us as our fingerprint and we suspect they are literally encoded in our DNA. For us, the question that most helps us get in touch with our sealed orders is this: What is the unique way I was created to give and receive love in this world? Jean Houston describes this as our essence:

> By "essence" I mean that part of our nature we recognize as the god in hiding, the source quality or soul quality that links us to our highest becoming, that transcends time and space, life and death.

This question about our essence or our unique way of giving and receiving love in this world has new meaning for us since the arrival of Dennis and Sheila's son, John Matthew, who was born just before we began this book. As we hold him, all three of us wonder why he came here. How will he be different from every other human being? What are his unique gifts and how can we help him fulfill the special purpose of his life? How can he live a life as fulfilling as that of his grandmother?

At eighty-six, John's grandmother suffers from considerable mental deterioration such that there are days when she doesn't know how to dress herself. Nevertheless, one morning each week she goes to a community center in the inner city of Minneapolis to teach reading to a man almost as old as she is who never went to school. She helped her own children learn to read, and when Dennis left home in 1962 she went back to school, became a developmental reading teacher, and has taught ever since. Her sealed orders have to do with learning and empowering others to learn by teaching them to read. The one thing she has asked us to do when she dies is to find another teacher for her student, Fred, to help him complete fourth grade.

One morning we introduced our friend, Char, to Mom. They had the following conversation:

*Char:* You were a teacher.
*Mom:* Not was.
*Char:* Oh, you *are* a teacher.
*Mom:* Yes. You are a teacher forever and ever.

Although on that day Mom taught no classes, her way of being in the world as a teacher informed everything she did, including her instructional way of responding to Char. *Being* a teacher gives meaning to Mom's life. How can we help John Matthew find his special way of being in the world that will give him a similar sense of meaning when he is eighty-six?

## What Matters Most Is a Meaningful Life

We often tell John Matthew that we don't want him to spend his time preparing for Advanced Kindergarten and then worrying about getting good grades so he will be accepted at the best universities and make a lot of money. Rather, we want him to ask himself every day how he can best carry out his sealed orders and contribute his unique gift to humanity. We tell him that if he does this and still needs help, we will provide for him. What we most want for John Matthew is a fulfilling, meaningful life.

We want to give John Matthew the freedom to choose those "doings" that will best express his special way of being—the same freedom that was given to us. For example, when we (Dennis and Matt) began our ministry of healing, our Jesuit provincial told us, "I don't know how to train you to be healers. But I want you to do anything and go anywhere that will help you to prepare yourselves. I will put all the resources of the Jesuits behind you." We took him at his word and went all over the world to learn about healing. Twenty years later, after giving retreats in over forty countries and writing sixteen books on healing, our ministry continues.

I (Sheila) attended a theological school that encouraged students to dream about who we wanted to become and then design our own educational program to prepare ourselves. I became interested in healing prayer soon after I entered, but there were no courses available on this topic. I contacted people who could guide me, created my own courses and got credit from my school. Students never received grades; instead, at the end of each semester, every student met with the entire faculty for a discussion of how that semester's work was contributing to his or her purpose in life.

We want to create a similar environment for John Matthew in which he is free to pursue the special purpose of his life, without having to make grades or financial success his primary focus. Doesn't God love each of us as much as we love John Matthew? If we want a fulfilling and meaningful life for John Matthew, doesn't God want the same for each one of us?

## CHAPTER 1

# *Meaninglessness Makes Us Sick and Meaningfulness Makes Us Well*

A general sense of meaning in life comes from a felt sense that we are living out the special meaning of *our* life. We live in a culture where many—perhaps most—people experience a lack of meaning in their lives and profound frustration over their seeming inability to live out their sealed orders. This lack of a sense of meaning, which seems to have reached epidemic proportions in our culture, affects us physically, emotionally and spiritually.

Physically, we suffer whenever we do anything that is not meaningful. For example, the most predictable factor for heart attacks is not cholesterol level, lack of exercise, smoking or even high blood pressure. The single greatest predictor for heart attacks is Monday morning. Most heart attacks occur Monday between 8:00 AM and 9:00 AM. Researchers believe this is because we face a week of work that we don't really want to do.

Not only our heart but our whole body suffers when our work is unfulfilling. When the Boeing Company studied the incidence of disabling back pain among its 31,200 Seattle employees, white collar workers pushing papers across their desks suffered as much as blue collar workers lifting heavy packages. It turned out that the best predictor for lower back pain was not physical exertion, but, rather, job dissatisfaction. Perhaps the prevalence of a sense of meaninglessness in the workplace is the reason why one of the most popular comic strips in America is "Dilbert." Millions of people seem to identify with Dilbert, as he toils in his shrinking office cubicle for an incompetent boss who thinks his dual-knobbed "Etch-a-Sketch" toy is really a complicated computer.

One person who has publicly articulated this frustration in the workplace is Michael Lerner, a political activist, psychologist and rabbi. He spent thirty years studying the concerns of working people and found that what they really want is not higher salaries or more benefits. Rather, their deepest concern is the lack of meaning and purpose they experience in their work. Thus Rabbi Lerner has begun a movement called the "Politics of Meaning," intended to make the bottom line in American public life meaning, caring and compassion rather than economic profit.

Meaninglessness affects us not only physically, as in the examples above from the workplace, but emotionally and spiritually as well. For example, Agnes Sanford's understanding of the importance of finding one's sealed orders grew out of her experience of recovery from years of depression. Her depression, at times suicidal, lifted only when she began to carry out her special purpose and found a deeper sense of meaning in her life. Looking back, she asked herself if God had sent her depression as a test:

> I do not think so. I think, rather, that God tried to show me the sealed orders with which I had come into the world, and I could not accept what He was trying to tell me. True, I had talents of writing, painting and drama, but I did not know that I also had a gift of healing. This gift is latent in everyone, but apparently in me it was a bit of a special gift, together with a special command, "This *do*."

Two of the greatest healers of our time, Carl Jung and Erik Erikson, would have understood Agnes' experience. The psychiatrist Jung claimed that after age 35, every emotional crisis is a spiritual crisis or crisis of meaning. Erik Erikson, the first major psychologist to say that we continue to develop throughout the entire life cycle, believed that mid-life crises are resolved when we discover a meaningful way to care for others—what he called "generativity."

The importance of meaning for emotional health is not just a mid-life phenomenon. According to Joseph Chilton Pearce, a brain spurt occurs in early adolescence related to the capacity for idealism. An adolescent's greatest developmental need is for adult models of a meaningful life who will encourage this idealism. If this capacity for idealism is not encouraged, millions of brain cells die and the young person experiences profound frustration. Instead of encouraging idealism, our educational system encourages adolescents to prepare themselves to participate in an economic system based on competition and profit at the expense of others. Rather than enhance each person's special way of *being*, this system promotes frenzied *doing*. Pearce suggests, and we agree, that our epidemic of teenage violence is a direct result of stunted brain growth and frustrated idealism caused by the lack of meaning adolescents perceive in the adult world that confronts them.

## Our Special Purpose Makes Us Well

Just as meaninglessness can make us sick, a sense of meaning and purpose in life can restore us to health at all levels. For example, Dr. Bernie Siegel found that he could predict which of his cancer patients would go into remission by asking

this question: "Do you want to live to be one hundred?" Those with a deep sense of meaning in their lives answered, "Yes," and they were the ones most likely to survive their illness.

What Bernie Siegel discovered is also evident in near-death experiences (NDE's). Those who return from such experiences typically bring with them a new and profound sense of their sealed orders or purpose in life. In his study of 350 adults who had NDE's, Dr. Melvin Morse describes how this sense of purpose brings healing at all levels:

People who have NDE's exercise more than the normal population, eat more fresh fruits and vegetables, use fewer medications like aspirin and other over-the-counter remedies. They also have fewer psychosomatic complaints, miss less time from work and have fewer years of unemployment than the control groups.

Also they have fewer hidden symptoms of depression and anxiety than any of the control groups. They spend more time alone in solitary pursuits or in meditation or quiet contemplation . . . give more of themselves to the community by performing volunteer work . . . give more of their income to charities and are often in helping professions like nursing or special education.

## Sealed Orders in Spirituality

Health crises like cancer or a near-death experience are extraordinary events that not all of us undergo. However, there are significant events common to many religious traditions that offer all believers an opportunity to find their purpose in life.

One example from Christian tradition is baptism. As we will discuss more fully in Chapter 8, we believe baptism is about sealed orders. When we celebrated John's baptism, we read Mark's account of Jesus' baptism, in which Jesus hears a voice from heaven saying, "This is my beloved Son in whom I delight" (Mk 1:11). Then we asked our eighty guests to get in touch with the special gifts they see in John that delight them. One after another, they came forward and blessed that special gift in John. One person, noticing John's ability to maintain eye contact for long periods of time, blessed his gift of intimate relationship. Others blessed his gifts of joy, focused awareness, having a quiet center, etc. John brought each of these gifts here with him and they are part of his sealed orders. The community's blessing upon these gifts was also a promise to support and encourage him for the rest of his life as he carries out his special purpose.

We hope John will have an abiding and increasingly clear sense of his sealed orders. If he loses his way, one thing that can help him is the *Spiritual Exercises*, the retreat process designed by St. Ignatius of Loyola to help those who want to find their special purpose. The *Spiritual Exercises* grew out of Ignatius' own experience of feeling lost and then finding his way. Ignatius had been a soldier who lived a wild life. He often daydreamed about the gallant deeds he would perform and the worldly glory he would obtain. Then, on the battlefield of Pamplona, a cannonball shattered his leg. During his recovery, Ignatius read a life of Christ and a book of the lives of the saints. As Ignatius meditated on what he read, he experienced consolation and he remained "cheerful and satisfied." As he meditated on the dreams of worldly glory that had previously enchanted him, he experienced desolation and felt "weary, dry and dissatisfied." As he pondered these two different movements of consolation and desolation, he discovered what we would call his sealed orders.

Ignatius was so healed and transformed by this discovery that he left behind his wild life and set off barefoot for Jerusalem. He eventually wrote the *Spiritual Exercises*, which have often been interpreted as designed to help the retreatant make significant life decisions or resolutions to improve what he or she is already doing. However, as Herbert Alphonso emphasizes, the goal of the *Exercises* is deeper and more far-reaching: it is to help each person find his or her special way of being that underlies all decisions and all activities.

If finding our sealed orders can be so healing, how do we do it? In this book we suggest some simple ways to begin, based upon our experience of the *Spiritual Exercises* and what we have learned from contemporary spirituality, psychology and medicine.

## CHAPTER 2

# Creating an Environment of Meaning and Purpose

We believe the best way to develop any positive quality in our lives, such as a sense of meaning and purpose, is to put ourselves in the presence of people and things that evoke that quality. No one of the three of us has ever felt that life was meaningless. Why not? Perhaps it is because each of us grew up in an environment where it was utterly evident that life is profoundly meaningful and that each of us is here for a special reason. It seems we "caught" a sense of meaning from our environment. In a similar way we want to create an environment for John in which he can "catch" a sense of meaning and purpose. Thus, the first thing we need to do for John to help him find the purpose of his life is to be in touch with our own. Perhaps as we share what we know thus far of our sealed orders, you will feel drawn to reflect on what you know of yours.

## Our Sealed Orders Are Revealed through the Circumstances of Our Lives

My favorite thing to do with John Matthew is take him outside into our garden and look at trees and leaves and flowers with him. As his big blue eyes grow even larger with wonder, I (Sheila) am reminded of what nourished me most when I was a small child.

I grew up in a home quite unlike the one Denny and I are trying to create for John. My parents were unable to provide a loving and secure environment for me. Thus I was a very insecure, shy and lonely child.

My refuge was a wooded area near our neighborhood. As I walked alone in those woods I would look at trees and leaves and flowers. These companions were

living beings to me and when I was with them I no longer felt alone. I loved them and I am quite sure that they loved me. I felt most truly myself during those times, and I think these early experiences of giving and receiving love with created things were my first glimpse of my sealed orders.

I believe my sealed orders are to cherish and care for created things, and by my care for them to reveal their goodness. I can't do otherwise. What began as one garden by the side of the house where Denny and I live has now extended to the front and the back, and I'm on my way up the hill into the thirty-four miles of national forest that adjoins our property. I am constitutionally unable to tolerate anything artificial in our home and even our measuring spoons are hand-made from natural wood. I need to be surrounded by natural things in which the goodness of creation is so evident to me.

Although it seems that my ministry is writing books and giving retreats, what I am actually doing as I work with people is finding the goodness in the process of human growth and revealing that goodness through my care for it. Denny's and my decision to have children grew partly out of my realization that for me raising a child is the ultimate way to care for created things.

My sealed orders of caring for created things were revealed through the circumstances of my early life and the way in which I relied upon trees and leaves and flowers for companionship as a shy and lonely child. Moreover, as I carry out my sealed orders, the hurtful aspects of my early life are more deeply healed. Every time I carry a bug outside and let it go, I am healing the ways I felt the life squashed out of me as a child. Every time I nurture a small seedling, I am nurturing the small child I once was.

Although we would not say that God sends our hurts, it does seem that God uses them to help reveal our sealed orders. Our sealed orders are built into us so deeply that difficult circumstances and mistakes in our life cannot ultimately keep us from carrying out our purpose. This is true because our purpose is our essence, a particular way the light of God shines within us, a light that can never really be put out.

## Following Our Sealed Orders Gives Life to the Whole World

I (Dennis) find that when I follow my sealed orders not only do I find healing and deeper life, but creative energy is released all around me. Thus, discovering and following my sealed orders is a way of caring for the whole world.

When I ask myself what my sealed orders might be, I think of two things. The first is how John came to us. Secondly, I think of my brother, Matt, who is holding John as I write this.

After trying to conceive during the first few years of our marriage, Sheila and I applied to adopt a baby. With our adoption agency's encouragement, we wrote to about five hundred friends all over the world asking them to watch and pray with us for the right child. We then began praying together each morning for the child that God was preparing for us. A year later we were still waiting.

One day we received an announcement in the mail about a workshop on birth trauma in Boulder, Colorado (two hours from our home). Neither of us had ever worked with birth trauma, but it occurred to us that this could be a way of empathically connecting with our child. Besides, we thought, if we experienced healing of our own birth trauma we would be less likely to pass on hurts to our child.

After two days of re-experiencing our own conception and birth at the workshop, we took a break and went to a local retreat house to pray about all that had happened so far. In the midst of our prayer Sheila said, "I think our baby has been conceived." As it turned out, Sheila was right. Although our child could have come from anywhere in the world, John Matthew came from Boulder. He was conceived at about the same time that we were re-experiencing our own conception and birth at the workshop there.

Although it may seem strange to those who have not experienced it, most workshop participants were able to re-experience their birth. They even felt they were able to go as far back as the time prior to conception, however one interprets their experience.

As I re-experienced my own conception and birth, I felt despair because I was leaving a loving God and coming into a family and religious culture that had a vengeful and punitive image of God. Those who believe in pre-existence, such as most of the other workshop participants, would say I was recalling my previous life in heaven. An orthodox Christian interpretation would be that I was longing for the love of God out of which I was created at the moment of conception.

Regardless of the explanation, what sustained me through this trauma was, from the moment of conception onward, communicating with my brother Matt. At the time of my conception Matt was about one year old and he could still remember heaven. I recently learned that traumatized babies in the womb, like myself, will often seek comfort from young siblings if their parents are unable to understand the trauma. Thus, I discovered that my close relationship with Matt began at conception.

It's no surprise to me that when I search for a word to describe my sealed orders, I think of "brother." As I reflect on my life, I see that no matter what I do, I am always looking for a way to be a brother. When I can't find it, I feel off-center and things don't go well. When I can find it, things go well for me and everyone around me.

For example, we invited all our five hundred friends to accompany us as brothers and sisters during the adoption process. I tried to become like a brother to John by attending the workshop and trying to experience some of the prenatal and birth trauma that he might be experiencing. Whether in my life as a Jesuit priest or now as a husband and father, I have always wanted to relate to others as a brother and equal, rather than as one who is in any way superior. Even now as I write, I am relating to you as a brother by trying to share my story with you.

I am constantly trying to find new ways to be a brother. What has most helped me to do this in the last few years is getting married and having a child. When I'm up in the middle of the night with my son, I feel like a brother to all the parents who have ever cared for a child in the night. Each time I discover another way of being a brother, new life comes to me, as in the case of the birth trauma workshop. Moreover, in some mysterious way, following my sealed orders unleashes creative love in the universe, the kind of love that gave birth to our son, John, in Boulder.

## Our Sealed Orders Help Us Discern the Next Step and Protect Us from Burnout

Making things whole has been central to my life as far back as I (Matt) can remember. As a child, when my mother called me and I didn't come in right away for dinner, it was because I was working on a puzzle and just about had the last pieces in place to complete it. If I wasn't doing that, I was playing with my doctor kit and diagnosing my teddy bear's ailments so I could make him well. In high school, my favorite activity was to be a negative debater diagnosing the world's ills and then presenting an airtight counterplan for how the issue could be resolved. I never really lost a debate, although the judges (who couldn't see the whole picture) thought I did.

I was going to be a doctor until I discovered that I could be a Jesuit priest who could make people whole not just physically but also emotionally and spiritually. In my seminary studies, I chose to focus on pastoral counseling. At various times, I was a hospital chaplain, high school teacher and missionary. Although it looks as if I've had different careers, each one has come from my unique, underlying sealed orders—my special way of being—which is to make things whole. For example, when I worked as a missionary among the Sioux Indians, I was always trying to put together the riches of their culture with our culture. Even as I taught Christian theology to the lay Sioux deacons, I encouraged them to integrate it with their own traditions so their religious experience would be more whole.

During my time with the Sioux, I learned about healing prayer. I saw that it could be integrated with the best of medicine and psychotherapy, and I settled on the healing ministry as a way to make things whole. Dennis and I began our ministry (later joined by Sheila) of giving retreats and writing books on healing.

My sealed orders to make things whole was not only the basis for choosing my ministry, but has more or less consciously informed every decision along the way. For example, six years ago my provincial asked if I would consider being the coordinator for a Minneapolis community of seventeen Jesuits. I calmly told him I wanted two weeks to pray about it, but inside I was quaking with fears. The previous coordinator had burned out after just one year of caring for a community member who was mentally ill and several others with various serious health problems. Furthermore, I could not always be physically present because I had already scheduled half my time away from Minneapolis giving retreats and writing with Dennis and Sheila. But, most of all, I feared that if I gave up the retreats and writing that give me so much life, I too would end up burned out in one year.

When I told my provincial the reasons why I could not take the job, he told me he had no one else. He asked if I would be willing to pray for two more weeks about what would make it possible for me to be coordinator. During those two weeks, I saw that my negativity had kept me from seeing how my gifts might be used in this role. I did love each person in the community and had a strong desire to make the community more whole.

But how could I continue retreats and writing when being community coordinator looked like a full-time job? What if I took the job, usually a six-year commitment, and after a year found myself stuck with something that was draining life from me? I tried to stay with my desire to respond to my provincial's need for help and at the same time with my inner sense of what gives me life.

Then it occurred to me that maybe I could find a way of being coordinator that wouldn't be full-time. Others could manage the finances and the upkeep of the house. I could ask someone to facilitate community meetings when I was gone.

In this way I would have enough free time to continue giving retreats and writing with Dennis and Sheila. It also occurred to me that I could accept the job on a trial basis, rather than making a six-year commitment. I agreed to try the job for one year. As it turned out, keeping up my ministry of writing and retreats has given me the life I need to protect myself from burnout, and I am now in my seventh year as community coordinator.

## *Sealed Orders as the Foremost Criteria of Discernment*

Our sealed orders, our unique way of giving and receiving life and love, are the foremost criteria of discernment for decision-making. Looking back on the month I spent agonizing over whether to accept the job as coordinator, I see that I could have reached my final decision much more easily by focusing on my sealed orders rather than on my fears. I could have started by naming my sealed orders and then measuring every aspect of my decision against them. As Herbert Alphonso writes,

> . . . the "personal vocation," once discerned, becomes *the criterion of discernment* for *every* decision in life, even for the daily details of decision-making. For my "personal vocation" is for me "God's will" in the deepest theological meaning of this much-repeated and much-misused phrase. If then I am faced with an option between two alternatives, it is my "personal vocation" that will help me decide through *discernment* which alternative is God's call, God's will *for me*. Checking the two alternatives separately over against the attitude of my "personal vocation," which I put on in depth, I can interiorly "experience" in a matter of minutes which alternative "fits in with" my personal vocation and which "jars over against it."

One implication of this is that so long as my decision "fit in with" rather than "jarred against" my personal vocation or sealed orders, I could rest assured that my decision would be a moral one and not a sinful one. As moral theologian Bernard Häring says, it is only when we grasp our unique identity that we can make a fundamental option for God's will in our lives. If a decision does not "fit in with" our unique identity, then it is "mortal" in the sense of bringing death to our deepest self and our unique calling.

Once we have made a decision, our "personal vocation" or sealed orders are

built into us so deeply and are so profoundly interwoven with God's evolving dream for the whole universe that if we stay with them they will lead us to a creative way to resolve seeming barriers to their fulfillment. Our sealed orders are our connection to our own life force, and when we follow them we receive what we need to overcome internal fears and external obstacles.

## *Sealed Orders Protect Us from Burnout*

Because our sealed orders are our connection to our own life force, following them not only helps us overcome fears and obstacles but also protects us from burnout. Burnout comes not from doing too many things, but from doing things that are not meaningful to us. However, those "doings" that we do find meaningful evoke the boundless energy of the life force within us. Put another way, our sealed orders come from God, and when we follow them we tap into the creative power of God. It is then that the same Spirit—the same power—that raised Jesus from the dead is at work within us (Rom 8:11).

If I had accepted the job of coordinator full-time and had agreed to use major amounts of my energy to manage the finances and upkeep of the house, I would have burned out. Although life requires all of us to sometimes do things that do not express our special way of being, burnout comes when we spend most of our time in this way. As David Steindl-Rast says, "The antidote to exhaustion is not necessarily rest. It's wholeheartedness." So long as I spend most of my time in ways that are wholehearted because they are true to my sealed orders, I doubt I will ever burn out.

### ⊗ HEALING PROCESS

**1.** Take a moment to grow quiet and breathe in the love of God.

**2.** Think of a person you know who lives a life that seems rich in meaning and purpose, and imagine yourself in the presence of that person. Breathe in the quality of a clear sense of direction that you feel with this person.

**3.** Now recall moments in your own life when you have felt a clear sense of direction. In your imagination, relive one of these moments. Breathe in again that clear sense of direction. As you do so, how might you begin to describe your sealed orders?

CHAPTER 3

# *What Are My Sealed Orders?*

If knowing our sealed orders can heal difficult circumstances in our past, create a loving environment in the world around us, help us discern the next step in our lives and protect us from burnout, how do we discover them? To help us get in touch with our sealed orders we light a candle, become aware of God's loving presence within us and take several minutes of quiet while we ask ourselves, "What is my unique way of giving and receiving love?" There are many other ways to ask this question:

When in your life have you been so
absorbed in something that time flew by?
For example, as a child what were you
doing when you were called for dinner
and came in late?

What are you most grateful for
today? What are you least grateful
for? If you were to ask yourself
these questions every day, what
pattern would you see?

When have you felt most alive, especially in
your body? What were the times of most life
that you would like to repeat?

What would you do if
you had time and money
to do anything?

What is the wildest thing you have done in your
life that turned out better than you ever imagined?
If you were assured of not failing, what is the
wildest thing you can imagine doing now?

Who is the person you most wanted to grow up to be like? Whom do you most want to be like today? Conversely, is there anyone you would like to mentor?

What movies or other stories have moved you most?

What do your best friends say they like about you? What do they see as your unique way of giving love?

What is your special way of receiving love?

What is it that you have to do— that you can't not do?

If you had only one year to live, what would you do?

*When in your life have you been so absorbed in something that time flew by? For example, as a child what were you doing when you were called for dinner and came in late?*

We first heard a similar question from Dr. Bernie Siegel, who has studied "exceptional cancer patients" and written extensively about the importance of love and meaning in recovery from cancer. As a child, when Bernie's mother called him for dinner and he didn't come right away, it was because he was totally absorbed in drawing portraits. Bernie wanted to *see* people—really see them. Now, when he treats a cancer patient, he doesn't just treat the cancer. Rather, he treats the whole person and he begins by trying to really *see* that person and what gives his or her life meaning. Bernie often recommends to his patients that they draw pictures as a way of getting in touch with the meaning of their illness and how it relates to their special purpose in life.

Our friend Mike, who comes from an upper-middle-class white family, recently graduated from a prestigious university and could easily have attended the best graduate program. Instead, he moved to Mississippi where he is teaching African American children in an impoverished school district. When Mike was four years old, what most absorbed him was giving speeches by Martin Luther King, Jr. He would climb up on the fireplace ledge at home and cry out, "I have a dream!"

When I (Dennis) was called for dinner and didn't come it was because I was reading books about far-away places. Every summer my parents turned Matt and me loose in the public library and told us we could plan a family trip. Matt and I would bring home travel books and plan a trip of five to seven thousand miles. In August, we and our parents would climb into the family car and I would tell my father, "Go right, go left, go straight." For three weeks, Matt and I led our parents all around the United States, Canada and Mexico. Traveling expanded my capacity to be brother so that I began to feel at home in strange places and with

strange people. (My mother, ever the teacher, always commented when we returned from these family trips, "It was a great education!")

As a Jesuit, I gave healing retreats in over forty countries. I realized only recently that according to the founder of the Jesuits, St. Ignatius, the first characteristic of a Jesuit is to travel. For me, travel has been a way of becoming a brother to the whole world.

Each of the above examples illustrates how the seed of our sealed orders can be evident even in early childhood. The seemingly trivial activities of children, including the ones that frustrate parents who have a warm dinner waiting on the table, can be preparation for that child's special purpose in life. We hope that as John grows we will consider the importance of what absorbs him before insisting he come right away for dinner.

Some of us may not be able to remember what we were doing as a child when we were called for dinner and came in late. But perhaps we can remember another moment when we were so absorbed in something that time flew by. Such experiences of timelessness are moments when we share, in a particularly pure and profound way, in the life of God in whom there is no time. It is precisely because our sealed orders were given to us by God from all eternity that moments of timelessness are moments when we are most living out our sealed orders.

&#9758; *What are you most grateful for today? What are you least grateful for? If you were to ask yourself these questions every day, what pattern would you see?*

These questions come from our adaptation of the Ignatian examination of conscience, which we call the "examen." The examination of conscience has something of a bad reputation, because it has often been interpreted as an exercise in finding one's sins and failings. However, we believe its real purpose is discernment. We wrote about how the examen can guide us in decision-making in our book *Sleeping with Bread*. We've found that if we do this process over time, it not only guides us in specific decisions but also reveals a pattern that underlies all our decisions. We believe that pattern is our sealed orders.

We do the examen together every evening. We light a candle, take a few minutes to grow quiet inside, and then ask ourselves the two examen questions. Then we share our answers. Last night all three of us were grateful for the same thing: the time we spent writing together yesterday. This often happens during the weeks we set aside for writing.

Each of us is grateful for writing for a different reason, and our reasons reflect our sealed orders. I (Sheila) like to draw out the hidden goodness in our topics. For example, on page 25 it was I who wrote about the hidden goodness in a child's seeming lack of cooperation at dinnertime. I (Matt) like to find the missing pieces in whatever we are writing and fill them in to make a whole. I feel delighted when I can churn out twenty pages in which no possible relevant point is overlooked. I (Dennis) want to communicate with our readers as a brother, and so I like to make things intimate and easy to relate to. I feel delighted when I can take Matt's twenty pages and reduce them to three that people like myself can understand.

What we are least grateful for also helps reveal our sealed orders. For example, last night all of us were least grateful that we have only two more days of writing. This tells us that writing is our priority and we need to eliminate some of the things that distract us from it—things we find distracting because they are *not* our sealed orders.

ꙮ   *When have you felt most alive, especially in your body? What were the times of most life that you would like to repeat?*

When we live out our sealed orders, we participate in the flow of life throughout the universe. As we said earlier, we believe our sealed orders are written on our DNA. Every cell of our body knows them. Thus a physically felt sense of aliveness is a sign that we are in touch with our sealed orders. Our sealed orders are the unique way we can best give and receive life with every cell, from our first breath to our last.

For example, since John was born we (Dennis and Sheila) sleep less than at any other time in our lives. We rarely get more than two or three uninterrupted hours of sleep before John wakes up to be fed and cuddled. At one level, we are chronically sleep-deprived and almost always tired. Yet, we also have more energy than at any other time in our lives. We, who both thought we could not function on less than eight hours of continuous sleep every night, find ourselves able to do twice as much in a day as we did before John came, and we do all of it more joyfully. Long after John begins sleeping through the entire night, we will look back on these early months as one of the most physically alive times in our lives. This sense of physical aliveness tells us that being parents is part of our sealed orders.

Because every cell of our bodies knows our sealed orders, our bodies are a fundamental means of discerning our special way of giving and receiving life. If we listen carefully, we will notice a physical shift or bodily felt sense of rightness and aliveness when we are on the track of our sealed orders. I (Sheila) experienced this as we waited for John. Before he came, we had several other babies offered to us. Each time, I felt a deadness in my body. As I tried to be with that deadness, I knew it was telling me, "You don't have life to give this baby because it's not *your* baby." The first time I heard about John, before we met him, I began sobbing. As I let myself be with the sobs, I felt my body exploding with life. I knew this feeling of aliveness was my body's recognition that John was ours. This process of being with feelings as they are carried in the body, known as "Focusing," is a way of discerning the sealed orders that are written on our DNA. Our sealed orders are the fundamental grace of our lives, and we can discern them by how this grace feels in our bodies.

*What would you do if you had time and money to do anything?*

If I (Sheila) had time and money to do anything, I would have more children . . . a *lot* more children. I don't remember not coming to dinner on time, but I do remember how absorbed I was in children when I myself was a child. For exam-

ple, one of my uncles took movies of my second birthday party. At the party I was surrounded by extended family members who brought several beautiful gifts. However, only one of them interested me: a doll that came with a bottle for feeding. I pushed away the other gifts and focused all my attention on feeding the doll. When Denny and I were deciding whether to have children of our own, I often watched those movies and the way in which even as a two-year-old I was so interested in caring for children. Now that we have John, I know that caring for life in the form of children is integral to my sealed orders. If our resources were unlimited, the first thing I would do is have a lot more children.

⊚  *What is the wildest thing you have done in your life that turned out better than
you ever imagined? If you were assured of not failing, what is the wildest thing
you can imagine doing now?*

Our friend Kate is a lovely, slender, artistic woman who lives in New York
City. A professional dancer, she has also studied theology and was ordained by her
church as a minister. Several years ago, during a difficult time in her marriage, Kate
felt helpless and unable to protect herself. When she asked herself what she most
wanted to do, she thought: "I want to be a cop."

Outrageous as it seemed, Kate completed the training and became an auxil-
iary police officer for the New York City Police Department. After she was hired
as a professor of dance at a college in the midwest, she became a part-time police
officer for the local police department. Her students were occasionally stunned to
find themselves pulled over by their dance professor in uniform when they were
out too late and drinking too much.

The empowerment Kate experienced through her police work contributed to
the healing of her marriage, and eventually she moved back to New York to rejoin
her husband. She is currently writing about issues of violence and vulnerability in
our culture, based upon what she learned during her years as a sensitive woman
immersed in the harsh world of criminal justice.

Once we asked Kate what the arts, theology and crime prevention have in
common. She answered, "They're all about how human beings get through the
night." We suspect Kate's answer was a summary of her sealed orders.

⊚  *Who is the person you most wanted to grow up to be like? Whom do you most
want to be like today? Conversely, is there anyone you would like to mentor?*

Sometimes we see in others what is as yet undeveloped in ourselves. For example, two of the guests who attended John's baptism were Dennis and Sheila's sixteen-year-old nephew, Loic, and our longtime close friend, Walter. Loic came from
Oregon and Walter came from Texas. These two formed an instant bond with one
another and spent long hours talking together on our deck. They've agreed to stay
in touch by telephone.

Walter is a psychotherapist, one of the finest we know. He is an extraordi-
narily perceptive and emotionally authentic person who brings a loving, affirming
presence into every situation. He is also extremely gifted in the area of spirituality. Loic has very similar gifts, that are still only partially known and not yet fully

developed. We suspect Loic's sealed orders may be somewhat like Walter's, and our guess is that this is the reason for his immediate sense of kinship with Walter. Moreover, Walter feels the same kinship with Loic.

Loic's desire to be like Walter when he grows up may be a sign of Loic's sealed orders. And Walter's desire to mentor Loic, a younger person who seems to have a similar call in life, may be a sign of *Walter's* sealed orders. We are often drawn to mentor in others those gifts that are similar to our own.

*What movies or other stories have moved you most?*

Dennis and Matt's mother doesn't especially like movies, yet she has watched *Mr. Holland's Opus* four times. This movie is the story of a music teacher who never completes his own musical opus because he is so busy helping his students develop their musical talent. We believe Mom's fascination with this movie flows from her own sealed orders to be a teacher who awakens the potential in her students.

If we list our five favorite movies or stories, we will probably find an underlying theme that is consistent with our sealed orders. If I (Matt) did this, my list would include *Schindler's List, Rain Man, Driving Miss Daisy, Gandhi,* and *Dead Man Walking.* Each of these movies has the underlying theme of making things whole through healing deep wounds . . . my sealed orders.

Just as we can use the stories in movies to evoke an awareness of our sealed orders, we can also use the stories in the Bible that move us most. For example, during Nelson Mandela's eighteen years of imprisonment in a seven-foot-square cell, he was sustained by the story of Jesus' passion and the words, "Father, forgive them for they know not what they do" (Lk 23:34). At Mandela's inauguration the presence of his former jailer, whom Mandela had forgiven, was a powerful symbol of his sealed orders of reconciliation that would dismantle centuries of apartheid.

*What do your best friends say they like about you? What do they see as your unique way of giving love?*

Sealed orders come with the gifts we need to carry them out. Sometimes our friends can see our gifts more clearly than we ourselves can see them. For example, each year we give a one-day workshop at the women's prison in Framingham, Massachusetts. The chaplain invited us to come because the women's greatest

problem is low self-esteem. This makes it hard for them to believe they have a con-
structive purpose in life and leaves them vulnerable to destructive influences. Low
self-esteem affects every fiber of these women's bodies. Their posture is poor, their
skin is sallow, their voices are thin and their eyes are full of fear and doubt.

    This past year, the theme of our day at the prison was affirming love. In the
afternoon, we asked for a volunteer. Kathy raised her hand and we invited her to
sit in front of the group, next to a blackboard. Nervously she agreed. Then we
asked the other eighty participants to tell Kathy the things they liked about her.
Although the atmosphere of prison life doesn't encourage such things, the other
women began to name Kathy's gifts. We wrote them on the blackboard and one
of the women made a copy on notebook paper for Kathy to keep.

    As Kathy heard the women list her gifts, her entire appearance changed. She
sat up straight and her skin began to glow. At the end we asked her how she felt.

She said, "There's a warm place in my heart and it's spreading all over my body." We asked Kathy to put her hand on the place in her body where the warmth was most intense and really allow herself to feel it. Then we said, "Whenever you feel badly about yourself, put your hand back on that place and remember the warm feeling." We were all so moved by the change in Kathy that we spent the rest of the afternoon repeating the process with one woman after another.

As we compared the lists of gifts, we were struck by the uniqueness of each list. Every woman in the prison has a special way of loving, which is her sealed orders. And each woman's gifts form the pattern of her sealed orders, much as the pieces of glass in a stained glass window form the pattern of its theme.

### ✆   *What is your special way of receiving love?*

We usually think of our sealed orders or our purpose in life as our special way of *giving* to others. However, as we hold seven-month-old John, we realize that our sealed orders are also our special way of receiving. John can't give anything more than a grateful smile or a happy burble when we feed him or change his diaper. Yet this past August, eighty people came to our home from as far away as the Philippines to pray for him at his baptism. Right now, John's purpose in life is to receive the love we and others have for him.

How we receive love is just as much a part of our sealed orders as how we give love. For example, Dr. Robert Coles tells the following story about his first meeting with Dorothy Day:

> It was on (an) afternoon, almost thirty-five years ago, that I first met Dorothy Day. She was sitting at a table, talking with a woman who was, I quickly realized, quite drunk, yet determined to carry on a conversation. The woman . . . had a large purple-red birthmark along the right side of her forehead. She kept touching it as she uttered one exclamatory remark after another, none of which seemed to get the slightest rise from the person sitting opposite her.
>
> I found myself increasingly confused by what seemed to be an interminable, essentially absurd exchange taking place between the two middle-aged women. When would it end—the alcoholic ranting and the silent nodding, occasionally interrupted by a brief question, which only served, maddeningly, to wind up the already overtalkative one rather than wind her down? Finally silence fell upon the room. Dorothy Day asked the woman if she would mind an interruption. She got up and came over to me. She said, "Are you waiting to talk with one of us?"

*One of us:* with those three words she had cut through layers of self-importance, a lifetime of bourgeois privilege, and scraped the hard bone of pride: "Vanity of vanities; all is vanity." With those three words, so quietly and politely spoken, she had indirectly told me what the Catholic Worker Movement is all about and what she herself was like.

If asked to describe Dorothy Day's sealed orders, most of us might say it was to give to the poor. However, this story demonstrates that her sealed orders were revealed as much by her ability to receive from them.

☙ *What is it that you* have *to do—that you can't* not *do?*

Sometimes we feel compelled to do something because we are addicted to it, such as the alcoholic who believes he or she *has* to drink. Other times we feel compelled to do something because it is what we were made for. For example, until she died in 1992 at eighty-seven, Clara Hale took in over one thousand babies born to drug-addicted mothers. She did this in her own home and at her own expense, often for as many as twenty babies at a time.

These babies spent their first weeks of life suffering from all the symptoms of drug withdrawal, such as shaking, vomiting and diarrhea. Clara said, "When a baby is crying for a drug, all I can do is hold it close and say to it, 'I love you and God loves you and your mama loves you. Your mama just needs a little time.'" When a television interviewer asked Clara why she devoted her life to troubled babies, she looked incredulous. She said, as if it should be obvious to anyone, "Honey, I was born to do this."

Clara Hale *had* to take in drug-addicted babies. I (Sheila) *had* to have a child. I (Denny) *had* to be a priest. I (Matt) also *had* to be a priest. As Frederick Buechner said, "The place God calls you is where your deep gladness and the world's deep hunger meet."

☙ *If you had only one year to live, what would you do?*

Sometimes it is only when we realize life is short that we do the most important things. Dr. Bernie Siegel tells the story of a man who wanted to be a violinist but instead became a lawyer in order to please his parents. He developed a brain tumor and was given only a year to live. He decided to spend his last year doing

what he really wanted. He quit law and devoted himself to playing the violin. A year later he had a job as a violinist in a concert orchestra and the brain tumor was gone.

Sometimes our answer to this question may be an obvious continuation of what we are already doing. For example, I (Matt) would keep giving healing retreats. Each year at Christmas, I (Dennis) write to all my friends telling them why I am glad to have them as a brother or a sister. If I had only a year left to live, I would make the letters longer. I (Sheila) would stay home to care for our son and study cooking. (Matt and Dennis, who love Sheila's cooking, would ask for a reprieve on all our death sentences.)

Sometimes our answer to this question may seem way beyond what we could possibly do. For example, during the last year of his life, Cardinal Joseph Bernardin initiated a project known as "Common Ground." His dream for this project was to initiate dialogue between different factions in the Roman Catholic Church. Four-fifths of the U.S. cardinals opposed him, and he was attacked by people on both sides. His dream of dialogue would certainly take years to carry out. Yet his credibility as a church leader and his vulnerability as a dying man made it difficult for anyone to refuse him. Even as he died he was carrying out what seemed to be his sealed orders: that of being a reconciler.

Whatever our answer to the question of what we would do if we had only a year left to live, we don't have to wait for a diagnosis of terminal cancer to do it. Our answer to this question may reveal our dream for the coming year. Each spring our friend, Dick Rice, travels to his home town to host his annual "Breakfast with Uncle Mick" (his nickname). All Dick's nieces and nephews eagerly attend, not just for the free breakfast but especially because they want to share their responses to the same annual topic, "What is my dream for this coming year?"

## ⚘ HEALING PROCESS

**1.** Take a moment to grow quiet and breathe in the love of God.

**2.** You may wish to imagine God speaking to you the words God spoke to Jeremiah:

> Before I formed you in the womb I knew you, and before you were born I consecrated you (Jer 1:5).

Imagine yourself with God, before you were born. You and God have been discussing the special purpose of your life and you have agreed to it. At the end of the conversation, God hands you an envelope containing your sealed orders.

**3.** What do you imagine is contained in the envelope? It may be helpful to ask yourself which of the above questions moved you most. Whichever one comes

to mind, see if your answer can help you discover what is in the envelope. Don't worry about an exact or specific answer, but rather trust whatever intuitions come to you no matter how partial and incomplete.

**4.** If you wish, continue your conversation with God. Is there anything God wants to say to you now about your sealed orders, or anything you want to say to God?

**5.** If possible, share as much of your sealed orders as you wish with a friend.

## What If You Don't Have a Name for Your Sealed Orders?

Perhaps the previous process helped you find a name for your sealed orders. If so, you are like our good friend, Francisco Miranda, the illustrator for our most recent books. After reading the rough draft for this one, he told us it confirmed his conviction that painting and sculpture are his special way of giving and receiving love. He felt more secure in his decision to move his family from Mexico City to Italy for eighteen months so that he can develop his skill with the unique white marble used by Michelangelo and found only there. Francisco can easily put his sealed orders into a few words: to discover and communicate beauty.

However, perhaps you have not been able to find a name for your sealed orders. If not, you are like Francisco's gifted wife, Beatriz. She finds it difficult to put into a few words her many ways of giving and receiving love: being a mother, sharing valuable moments with her husband and loved ones, teaching English to children, watching nature, listening to music, traveling. Yet Beatriz knows intuitively when what she is doing is true to her unique vocation, even if she can't summarize her vocation in a few words. When we have varied talents, we may find it more difficult to identify our underlying sealed orders.

Finding a name for our special purpose may take a lifetime because each of us is a multi-faceted mystery. Or a name that fits our special purpose at one time in our life may no longer seem quite right a few years later, as our understanding of our purpose deepens and evolves. For example, at various times in my life I (Dennis) have described my sealed orders as "community builder," "healer," "still waters," "dancing heart," and "ecstasy." Now "brother" seems to encompass all these facets of my sealed orders.

Perhaps discovering our sealed orders is like trying to define why we want to marry the person we choose as our life partner. We intuitively know what is special about this person, even if we cannot put it into words. Whatever we *could* put into words would be true yet incomplete. After twenty years of marriage, we know our partner at greater depth and from many more aspects. We could add to our earlier description of our partner's specialness (which remains true), but even this fuller description would still be incomplete.

So, if you still find it difficult to describe your sealed orders, perhaps it is because you intuitively know that the evolving mystery of your life cannot adequately be put into words at this time. As Herbert Alphonso writes,

> . . . what is most personal is incommunicable. Personal knowledge, or what St. Ignatius repeatedly in the *Exercises* so admirably calls 'interior knowledge,' is not conceptual knowledge; it is a knowledge of the heart. We can put into words only what we can put into concepts. This is why in sharing a profound personal experience, we can at best approximate to capturing it in poor inadequate human language. Is it surprising that when it comes to formulating what we have discovered as our God-given uniqueness—that is, our profoundest personal experience—we capture it in inadequate human words which sound exteriorly very general, but which speak to us in fact, at the core of our being, of our deepest and truest 'self,' of our unrepeatable uniqueness?

The important thing is to love our uniqueness, whether we can put it into words or not. As we do so, our sealed orders will animate all that we do and point us in the direction of ever deeper life.

CHAPTER 4

# *Love Empowers Us To Carry Out Our Sealed Orders*

Maybe you still aren't sure about your purpose in life. However, let's imagine you have answered all the questions in the last chapter in such a way that your sealed orders are now crystal-clear to you. Does that mean you will feel able to carry them out? Not necessarily.

The power to be our real self and to accomplish something in life comes not so much from knowing who we are and what it is we want to do, but rather from feeling loved enough to be and do it. For example, Dr. William Miller did a study of the effect of psychotherapy on alcoholics. He randomly assigned problem drinkers to receive six to eighteen weeks of outpatient therapy. Members of a control group saw a counselor for only one session and were sent home with self-help resources. To Dr. Miller's horror, those in the control group improved as much as those in treatment. These results so violated his training that he repeated the study four more times in three different states, always with the same results.

Finally, by chance, a measure of the empathy level of the therapists was included in the study. The nine therapists in the study were each ranked by supervisors according to their capacity to be empathically present (i.e., to communicate love) to the client, without giving advice or conveying judgment. The therapist whom supervisors agreed was the most empathic had a one hundred percent success rate in helping her clients stop drinking, while the least empathic therapist had a twenty percent success rate. Dr. Miller and his colleagues discovered they could predict how much their clients would drink six months later solely on the basis of the therapist's capacity for empathy. The more empathic the therapist, the less the client would drink. Even two years later, the inverse correlation between therapist empathy and the client's number of drinks per week was very high.

## *Near-Death Experiences and Sealed Orders*

Dr. Miller's research demonstrates that even when we know what we want to do, such as stop drinking, we can't do it unless we feel loved. Perhaps the most powerful evidence of the power of love to help us carry out our purpose in life comes from near-death experiences (NDE's). There are several typical elements in NDE's, but the critical one is meeting with an unconditionally loving Being of Light. This meeting results in a deep personality transformation such that the person no longer fears death. As mentioned in Chapter 1, the person also experiences a new and profound sense of his or her sealed orders or purpose in life as well as the power to carry them out.

Dr. Melvin Morse gives the example of Annie, a depressed sixteen-year-old who experimented with drugs, alcohol and sex. When her boyfriend found another girl, Annie decided to commit suicide. In imitation of her mother's suicide a few years earlier, Annie overdosed on barbiturates and vodka. While her friends tried to revive her Annie had the following experience, which she described many years later:

> It took me a while to realize that I was out of my body and floating up by the ceiling. I wasn't alone. There was someone else there, a Guardian Angel or something. We were both made of light. I felt three-dimensional and I seemed to be made of something that wasn't solid, maybe gelatin. . . .
>
> The angel didn't speak, but it communicated. I was shown the beauty of my body and of every body. I was told that my body was a gift and I was supposed to take care of it, not kill it. After hearing this, I felt very, very ashamed of what I had done and hoped that I would live. I began to beg the light for life. The feeling that came back was the strongest feeling of love I have ever experienced, even more than the feeling of love I have for my own children.

Immediately after she came back to life, Annie stopped her wild lifestyle and found a new set of friends. Now, more than twenty years later, Annie is happily married and has four children. Looking back on her NDE she says,

> Immediately after the experience I felt as though I had been given a mission in life, like I was born to accomplish something. The experience gave me an inner energy that has never left me.

Annie's experience of finding her mission in life and feeling empowered by love to carry it out is typical of those who survive NDE's. This is true even for those who despair of finding meaning in life and attempt suicide. For example, Dr. Bruce Greyson has studied hundreds of suicide attempts. He compared those who had near-death experiences during their suicide attempt with those who did not, and followed them over several years. Those who do not have an NDE have a high rate of continued suicide attempts. However, those who do have an NDE virtually never again attempt suicide. When asked why they choose to live, these people say it is not because they fear they will be cast into hell if they try to kill themselves again. Rather, like Annie, they say their near-death experience of the loving Being of Light taught them that life has a purpose and empowered them to live it out.

A famous example of the power of NDE's may be Cardinal John Henry Newman. Although we cannot be certain, the circumstances of his near-fatal illness during a trip to Sicily in 1833 suggest an NDE. After that illness, he wrote frequently of an unconditionally loving "Kindly Light" that was leading him. He returned to England certain that God had a special mission for him there, and he wrote:

> God has created me to do Him some definite service; He has committed some work to me which He has not committed to another. I have my mission—I may never know it in this life, but I shall be told it in the next. . . . Therefore I will trust Him. Whatever, wherever, I am, I can never be thrown away. If I am in sickness, my sickness may serve Him; in perplexity, my perplexity may serve Him; if I am in sorrow, my sorrow may serve Him.

Newman is known for the warmth of his spirituality and his courage in resisting institutional pressure in order to follow his own conscience—his perception of the "Kindly Light." Perhaps it was a near-death experience that released these qualities in him.

What is it about the NDE that makes it so powerful? The essential element is feeling loved unconditionally by the Being of Light. In the compassionate presence of the Being of Light, the person feels freed from the negative effects of past hurts and mistakes. The Being of Light's love is so powerful that even the physiological effects of emotional trauma on the brain are healed.

The hurts we suffer and the guilt we feel over the mistakes we have made with others tend to disconnect us from a felt sense of our real self and its goodness. The Being of Light's love seems to be rather like a laser beam that penetrates to the core of the person restoring contact with his or her essence. This essence *is* the primary meaning of sealed orders—it is our special way of being. When we are in touch with our special way of being, the power to act accordingly comes naturally.

## Opening Ourselves to Unconditional Love

Not all of us have had a near-death experience and we cannot manufacture one for ourselves. However, perhaps we can learn something from NDE's about the power of unconditional love to help us carry out the purpose of our life. Those who have had NDE's say that the quality of love they experienced is infinitely beyond anything they have known in this world. Yet it is the same love from which we originally came and it hovers over us throughout our lives. Apparently the limitations of life on earth make it difficult for most of us to experience this love in all its intensity. But we can at least open ourselves to it and grow in our capacity to take it in. As we do so, our capacity to carry out our special way of loving, which is our sealed orders, also grows.

For example, I (Dennis) was a very scrupulous adolescent whose primary goal in life was avoiding hell. I tried to avoid the long list of sins I had been taught would surely lead to eternal banishment. Because of my scrupulosity I hated myself and didn't like anyone else either.

The main change in my life happened thirty-five years ago after I joined the Jesuits. At that time, our novice master, Joe Sheehan, instructed us to make a general confession of all the sins of our life. I wrote twelve pages of all the things I didn't like about myself. I gave the twelve pages to Joe, hoping he would read them during his free time and later give me absolution. Instead, he asked me to tell Jesus aloud everything I wanted to confess. I started with page one and talked non-stop for thirty minutes.

What I remember most is the hug Joe gave me at the end. With that hug I knew God loved me whether I ever changed or not. I felt like the woman who washed Jesus' feet with her tears and dried them with her hair. As Jesus told the Pharisees, "That woman can love a lot because she has been forgiven a lot" (Lk 7:48). Ever since that moment, I have loved myself and almost everyone else as well. I have felt that I could be a brother to all people, that I could love a lot because I have been forgiven a lot—at least twelve pages worth! Although I have never had an NDE or met the Being of Light, I do know that in the hug Joe Sheehan gave me I experienced the unconditional love of God. I felt empowered to carry out my sealed orders of being a brother to all.

For some of us, the love that frees us may come through a hug at just the right moment from a mentor like Joe Sheehan or from a friend. For others of us, it may come from an empathic therapist like those in Dr. Miller's study. For others, like Sheila, it may come from nature. The infinite love of God from which we came and that hovers over us will touch us in any way it can. A number of us have heard so many "No's" in our life that we need someone or something that can express to us God's radical "Yes" to who we really are. As Kaylin Haught writes:

### *God Says Yes To Me*

I asked God if it was okay to be melodramatic
and she said yes
I asked her if it was okay to be short
and she said it sure is
I asked her if I could wear nail polish
and she said honey
she calls me that sometimes
she said you can do just exactly
what you want to
thanks God I said
and is it even okay if I dont paragraph
my letters
Sweetcakes God said
who knows where she picked that up
what I'm telling you is
Yes Yes Yes

### ☙ HEALING PROCESS

**1.** Light a candle (or imagine one) and breathe in the creative light of God. Take a moment to grow quiet within.

**2.** Once again, imagine yourself with God, before you were born. Imagine that you and God have been discussing the special purpose of your life and you have agreed to it. Imagine that at the end of the conversation, God hands you an envelope containing your sealed orders and sends you forth to live them out.

**3.** In your imagination, see yourself as you are now. Hold the envelope in your hands. Ask yourself whose love would empower you to carry out the mission contained in the envelope. Who says God's "Yes" to you?

**4.** Whoever comes to mind, see yourself in the presence of that person and breathe in his or her love for you. Perhaps, instead of a person, you will see yourself next to a favorite tree or by a stream that always fills you with new life.

**5.** If you find it helpful, allow the love you feel to expand until it is as big as the infinite love of God for which this person or natural object is a channel.

**6.** As you breathe in this love, imagine yourself carrying out your sealed orders.

**7.** If you wish, find a way to spend extra time in the presence of this person or natural setting.

## CHAPTER 5

# We Can Catch Our Sealed Orders from Others

In Chapter 4, I (Dennis) told the story of the general confession I made with Joe Sheehan when I first entered the Jesuits. Joe was an extraordinary Jesuit. At a time when hierarchy was still strongly emphasized in religious life, Joe treated novices like brothers and equal friends. Although he was much older, he joined us in everything from chores to soccer games. The hug he gave me was so healing, in part, because it was so extraordinary. In those days, priests didn't hug. Joe was the kind of priest I wanted to be. Because he knew how to be a brother, I believe my sealed orders of being a brother were nurtured by his love for me. I stayed as close to Joe as I could throughout my training, and a few years ago I traveled twenty-five hundred miles to make a retreat with him.

Because we believe our sealed orders need to be modeled and nurtured by others, the three of us often go far out of our way to be with people who can do that for us. For example, after we (Dennis and Sheila) were married, we moved to a small mountain community in Colorado. Since we write at home and give retreats all over the world, we could live anywhere. Why did we choose to live in a ski resort? We don't even ski!

For several years prior to our marriage our friends, Paul and Sally, who own a hotel in this community, had given us free rooms in the summer so that we and Matt could write in a beautiful environment. We always noticed how, after many years together, Paul and Sally's relationship still sparkled. Their model of marriage is based on deep friendship and presumes equality between men and women, a value that we share.

As a newly married couple, we wanted to establish the foundation for a happy marriage. Since we believe we "catch" things from other people, our first question in deciding where to live was, "Who are the happiest married couples we

know?" One of the couples we thought of immediately was Paul and Sally and, as it turned out, we were given most of the value of a home two miles from theirs. Part of our sealed orders is to be married to each other, and we have "caught" the ability to carry this out in part from Paul and Sally, who are married to each other in a way we admire.

Several of the guests at John's baptism traveled a thousand miles from St. Louis to be with us. These friends belong to a group that first formed at the time of our engagement and that gathers again once every year as we make a special visit to St. Louis. We first met in St. Louis and have many friends there. In the fall of 1989, we gathered twenty-five of those friends together for an engagement party. We had a prayer service at which we told each individual what gift we needed from him or her to carry out the sealed orders of our marriage. For example, Jim and Mary Jo have a strong, shared commitment to social justice. Part of the sealed orders of their marriage seems to be to reach out to the poor as far away as Nicaragua, where they have traveled with their children to help set up a women's co-op. We want this same gift in our marriage and we asked Jim and Mary Jo to bless us with it. They do this again each year when our St. Louis group gathers for its annual reunion.

The people from whom we catch our sealed orders may have lived before we were even born. Perhaps they were our ancestors, as we'll discuss in Chapter 6. Perhaps they were authors who seem like beloved friends as we read their books. For example, I (Sheila) learned to see nature as a "Thou" from Martin Buber, the Jewish theologian who said we can have an "I-Thou" relationship with all of creation. My special companion as a Roman Catholic has been St. Thomas Aquinas, who saw nature as revelatory of God and loved "the warmth of the wonder of created things."

## *Perhaps Our Special Companions Were Sent with Us*

How is it that we find friends like those in our St. Louis group who feel so "right" and who naturally know how to help us carry out our sealed orders? How did Joe Sheehan, a person with whom Dennis resonates so deeply, end up in Dennis' Jesuit community as his novice master? How did Matt and Dennis, whose sealed orders so perfectly complement one another, end up in the same family? How did Sheila and Dennis, whose marriage so wonderfully helps each to carry out their sealed orders as individuals and as a couple, ever find each other? Often

we think that as we go through life we "happen" to meet people who can help us on our way.

But what if our special companions were sent here with us in the first place? Just as God sent John the Baptist ahead with sealed orders to prepare the way for Jesus, what if God sends people along with every one of us? What if the resonance we feel when we meet such a person is a recognition of someone who was sent to help us, just as John the Baptist recognized Jesus and leapt while they were both still in the womb?

### ✒ HEALING PROCESS

**1.** Take a moment to grow quiet within and breathe in the love of God. Get in touch with as much as you know at this time of your sealed orders.

**2.** As you imagine yourself coming into this world carrying your sealed orders, ask if there is anyone else God sent with you or perhaps ahead of you to inspire and encourage you. This person might be a teacher, a colleague, your spouse, an author, an ancestor, your favorite saint, a figure in the Bible, etc. Perhaps you will think of several people.

What is each one's special gift with which you want him or her to bless you?

**3.** Imagine yourself with that person or persons and see them giving you what you most need in order to live out your sealed orders. Then see yourself actually living out your sealed orders in some way, even if it seems to be only a small and beginning way.

**4.** If you wish, spend some time with the person or persons you believe God sent here to inspire you.

CHAPTER 6

# We Can Catch Our Sealed Orders from the Earth

As I (Sheila) described in Chapter 1, when I was a child my refuge from a troubled family was a wooded area near my home. As I walked in those woods, often I would notice a particular leaf or a blade of grass. I sat for what seemed like hours looking at that leaf or blade of grass, noticing how utterly good it was. The leaf or blade of grass would become like a window to something larger than itself—a presence. That presence was personal and it was loving. Sometimes at a certain point there was a shift. I sensed that presence looking back at me through the leaf or the blade of grass, as if it were trying to tell me how good *I* was and that I was here for a special purpose. In those moments I felt *seen* by nature as myself. I believe my sealed orders are to do for all creation what nature did for me: to *see* it for its own sake, to recognize how good it is and that each thing is here for a special purpose.

## Affinity with Nature Is Innate

Hopefully the home we (Dennis and Sheila) are providing for John is more secure and loving than was Sheila's, yet he is drawn to nature also. Sometimes when he cries it is not because he's hungry or tired, but because he wants to go outside. As soon as the door closes behind him and he feels the fresh air on his skin, he stops crying. Our friends have given him many plastic toys, yet his favorites are made from natural materials. He loves to play with straw baskets and wooden spoons. He has a styrofoam ball, but he much prefers to roll apples or oranges.

One day a friend brought some flowers and we placed them in a vase on the kitchen counter. John's whole body went into a state of ecstasy as he gazed intently

50

at the flowers. He reached out to them as if wanting to incorporate them all into himself. We gave him one, which he promptly ate. Since then, one of his favorite stops on his crawling route is the pot of geraniums in the corner of the living room.

We believe all children come here with the same affinity for nature that is so evident in John. Children have an innate sense of wholesome relationship to created things, such as foods. As Dr. Benjamin Spock writes, "children have a remarkable inborn mechanism that lets them know how much food and which types of food they need for normal growth and development." If this inborn mechanism is not tampered with and if they are allowed to decide for themselves what they want to eat and when, even very small children who are offered a variety of foods will choose a balanced diet. Perhaps this is because, as Brian Swimme says,

> . . . eating is remembering. . . . Many of our physiological patterns of activity depend on certain complex chemicals provided by natural foods. The physiological processes are the way the body remembers its ancestral heritage, and this heritage insists on particular natural foods for its remembering. When you eat grains, legumes and good, fresh meat and vegetables, you enable your body to remember its powers.
>
> It is similar to what happens when you leaf through an old photo album. The pictures key all sorts of memories, and you are flooded with the past coming alive within you.

Like food, Swimme says that exercise, too, is remembering:

> When we exercise, we bring into action our ancestral memories. Our bodies remember that we lived in trees and forests. We need to crawl and climb and run if we are to develop our intellectual, emotional and spiritual capacities.

If eating and exercising are remembering where we came from, how is it that so many of us have forgotten? Children's innate wisdom about wholesome food can be damaged in many ways, such as by eating an artificial food like sugar. Similarly, our innate wisdom about wholesome sounds, textures and images can be damaged by traffic noises, mass-produced synthetic objects and electronic television pictures. These artificial sense experiences can confuse our ability to recognize and appreciate natural ones. By the time most of us grow up, we have lost our connection to nature and find it hard to hear its voice. Yet, as in Sheila's example, nature can reveal to us our sealed orders.

### Our Ancestors Are More Than Human

We (Dennis & Matt) found part of our sealed orders when we visited our mother's ancestral home in Glendalough, Ireland. As we entered St. Kevin's Church, we found it full of people praying. We watched the grandparents praying for their children and grandchildren. We also felt the unseen presence of many generations of people who had prayed there and realized that they, too, were interceding for their descendants. We thanked God for our ancestors and asked them to intercede for us to receive all the good that is in our mother's family line. In the five years before this trip, we had given retreats in five countries. In the five years afterward, we gave retreats in thirty countries. Looking back, we realize that it was from Glendalough that the Irish monks set out to bring Jesus' healing love to Europe and the known world. These monks specialized in reconciliation and healing, as we do.

We believe that human ancestors, such as Dennis and Matt's from Glendalough, can help us find our sealed orders. However, as James Hillman says, our ancestors are more than human:

> In other societies, an ancestor could be a tree, a bear, a salmon, a member of the dead, a spirit in a dream, a special and spooky place. . . . Ancestors are not bound to human bodies and certainly not confined to physical antecedents whose descent into your sphere was allowed only by your natural family.

Perhaps this is why so often when we enter a forest or sit by a stream we feel that we have come home to ourselves.

Many people who have lost their way in life have been able to regain it through contact with nature. For example, troubled adolescents have been helped through participation in the Outward Bound program where they are immersed in the wilderness and finally spend twenty-four hours alone listening to nature. Similarly, Catherine Sneed began a gardening program for prisoners in the San Francisco County jail. As they learn to nurture small seedlings, many of the prisoners begin to see all of life as deserving of nurture. They can no longer harm others or themselves, and many have been able to use the gardening skills they learned in prison to find meaningful work on the outside. Dr. Karl Menninger did something comparable for psychiatric patients at the Menninger Clinic in Topeka, when he instituted gardening therapy. Sometimes nature can help us find our way in life when human beings alone cannot. All of creation has something to pass on to us:

> As far back as we can imagine cultural history, it was widely believed that animals were the first teachers. Our earliest language, our dances, our rituals, our knowledge of what to eat and what not to eat, passed into our behavior through theirs.

This awareness of nature having something to teach us was shared by Jesus. Many of his parables use examples from nature to instruct his listeners, such as the one encouraging us not to worry but to "Think of the ravens. They do not sow or reap; they have no storehouses and no barns; yet God feeds them" (Lk 12:24). Jesus came from a long line of Jews who experienced God's guidance through burning bushes, clouds, etc.

The greatest theologian of the church, St. Thomas Aquinas, spoke of two sources of revelation for Christians: the Bible and nature. He said that every creature is *actively* revealing God to us, luminous with God's presence and crying out to us of God's goodness. In the Bible, the Greek word used for God's glory is *doxa*, meaning the divine radiance of God in all creation. Modern science has confirmed the truth of this, with the discovery that every created thing contains photons which are the source of light and literally radiant. David Bohm, one of the foremost physicists of the twentieth century, referred to matter as "frozen light." St. Ignatius must have understood this in his own way, since the foundation of Ignatian spirituality is finding the presence of God in all things.

## *God Can Speak to Us through the Earth*

In our own lives, God has sometimes spoken through animals and other things of the earth to help us discover our sealed orders. For example, when I (Dennis) was discerning whether to marry Sheila, I made a thirty-day retreat at a Jesuit retreat house in Ontario. Being a Jesuit priest, I had a very serious decision facing me, and I wanted to be responsible to the commitments I had made to the Jesuits and to the larger Christian community.

I also had two fears that made it difficult for me to hear whether marriage was part of my sealed orders. I was afraid of offending people who might disapprove if I decided to marry, and I was afraid of practical things I had never had to do as a Jesuit priest, such as earn a living and pay taxes.

The shadow side of my sealed orders of being brother is wanting to bend over backwards to be a brother to everyone under all circumstances, and to never offend anyone. All the gifts that come with our sealed orders also form the shadow side of our personality when we overuse or underuse them. For years I had been drawn to tall trees, as if they could teach me how to be a brother while maintaining the strength and courage I felt I lacked. During this retreat, whenever I was in touch with my fear of offending others, I spent long periods looking at tall trees. Each day as I considered the various options of what I might do, one question I asked myself was what would help me that day to become like a tall tree. I wanted to become used to feeling like a tall tree. Ultimately I knew that part of the basis of my decision about marriage would be whatever would match this feeling and thus help me grow more deeply rooted in my sealed orders and less easily blown over by others . . . like a tall tree.

My other fear was of the practical responsibilities of marriage. One day as I sat before a large window watching the snow fall gently on farm fields, the peace

of the snowy scene came inside me. The peaceful fields seemed to be saying to me, "We are your brothers and your sisters. Just as we have been cared for all these years, so will you." I felt a change throughout my body—my back seemed to straighten and I felt taller. It was as if every cell believed the message of the peaceful fields. I could now consider marriage freely. (Now, each year when income tax season comes, I return to that snowy scene!) I could have spent years trying to heal all the hurts behind my fears, but I doubt I would have received what was given to me by nature in those few moments.

I finally decided that my sealed orders included marriage, and in 1989 Sheila and I were married. After several years of trying to conceive, we considered adoption. One afternoon we sat in our backyard, in touch with all our fears of adopting a child. A deer came down the hill and stopped about ten feet away from us. It stood and looked at us for a very long time, as if intent on communicating something. We both had the sense that it was bringing a message from Denny's father, who loved deer and who had died the previous month. He seemed to be saying, "Don't be afraid. Go ahead."

The next day we called a local adoption agency and told them we were ready. While we waited for a child, we began a small addition on our house. The house was originally designed for guests and not for children. The addition was a way of letting matter—cement and wood and nails—express our dream for a child. The construction was done by friends who could come for only short periods each week and so the project took nearly a year. We recalled the words from the movie *Field of Dreams*, "If you build it, he will come." We found ourselves answering people who asked about our adoption process, "Our child will come when the addition is finished." On May 20 we passed the final building inspection. On May 22 the adoption agency told us John was ready to be released. We brought him home that night.

## *Mother Nature Is Part of Our Sealed Orders*

In the above experiences of discerning a marriage or waiting for a child, natural things were intimately involved in revealing our sealed orders to us and helping us carry them out. Conversely, it seems to us that any authentic understanding of our sealed orders will involve care for the earth, directly or indirectly. Our sealed orders come from God. Since the earth is full of God's presence, God will not send us here to do anything that would violate that presence. The earth is also our

source, since we evolved from it. We are the rainforest and the lakes and the air become conscious of themselves. Part of our sealed orders is to speak for them.

Our generation may have a special responsibility to recognize our kinship with all of life. As James Hillman says, ecological disaster comes from the belief

> . . . that what's out there is less of a factor than my close family in the formation of who I am. . . . Until this psychological fallacy is set straight, no compassionate campaigns of multi-culturalism and environmentalism, no field trips, Peace Corps, bird-watching or whale songs can fundamentally reattach me to the world.

The point of this chapter is that one way to find our sealed orders is to listen to those parts of nature with which we feel a special attachment or kinship. And a sign that we have heard our sealed orders rightly is that carrying them out will be consistent with care for the earth.

The earth is in such great danger today that we may ask ourselves what difference our small contribution can make. Archbishop Raymond Hunthausen, formerly of Seattle, had a favorite story about a coal mouse bird and a wild dove that sustained him when he felt discouraged:

> "Tell me the weight of a snowflake," a coal mouse asked a wild dove.
> "Nothing more than nothing," was the answer.
> "In that case I must tell you a marvelous story," the coal mouse said. "I sat on a branch of a fir, close to its trunk, when it began to snow—not heavily, not in a giant blizzard, no, just like in a dream, without any violence. Since I didn't have anything better to do, I counted the snowflakes settling on the twigs

and needles of my branch. Their number was exactly 3,741,952. When the next snowflake dropped onto the branch—nothing more than nothing, as you say—the branch broke off."

Having said that, the coal mouse flew away. The dove, since Noah's time an authority on the matter, thought about the story for a while and finally said to herself: "Perhaps there is only one person's voice lacking for peace to come about in the world."

## ⊛ Healing Process

**1.** Take a moment to grow quiet within and breathe in the love of God. Get in touch with as much as you know at this time of your sealed orders.

**2.** As you imagine yourself coming into this world carrying your sealed orders, ask yourself if there is any other creature or natural setting God sent with you or perhaps ahead of you to inspire and encourage you. This might be an animal, a favorite tree, a stream, a stone, a special corner of your backyard, or any place where you feel one with nature.

What is each one's special gift with which you want them to encourage and bless you?

**3.** Imagine yourself with that creature or in that natural setting and see it giving you what you most need in order to live out your sealed orders. Then see yourself actually living out your sealed orders in some way, even if it seems only a small and beginning way.

**4.** If possible spend some time with that creature or in that place you believe God sent here to inspire you.

CHAPTER 7

# *Healing Hurts*

If none of us were ever hurt, we imagine we would all be entirely free to give and receive the love of God in our unique way. Life—and our special purpose in life—could flow freely through us. However, even John, who is only a few months old, has already experienced some hurts. Several frightening and traumatic things happened during his time in the womb. He was born prematurely and subjected to highly invasive medical tests. When John first came to us as a newborn, his hands and feet were tightly clenched, as if trying to pull away from things that might hurt him again. His body was an image of how hurts affect us. They constrict our whole being so that life no longer flows freely through us. Our energy is taken up with self-defense and we have little left to carry out our purpose in life. When our hurts are healed, as we've seen happen in John, the constriction leaves us and our unique potential can unfold.

Perhaps one reason near-death experiences are so transformative and release so much human potential is that they include healing of hurts. NDE's often include a review of one's past life with all its hurts and mistakes in the presence of the unconditionally loving Being of Light. Although we cannot on our own create the laser-beam-like healing effect of an NDE, we can experience healing of our hurts to the extent we let them be touched by unconditional love.

For example, Daddy King, the father of Martin Luther King, Jr., grew up hating white people. As a child he played with the children of the white family for whom his mother worked as a cleaning woman. However, when it came time for meals, the white children went inside to the dining room and Daddy King had to eat alone on the back steps. As early as age three, he resolved to hate these white people who humiliated him. When he was fifteen he walked into a church, looked

up at the cross and heard Jesus say, "Love your enemies; do good to those who hate you." His hatred was melted by love and in tears he began to forgive white people.

Daddy King passed on this ability to forgive racial hurts to his son, Martin, who in turn founded the Civil Rights Movement based on non-violence and forgiveness. When Martin Luther King, Jr., was murdered, his vision of peace could easily have been destroyed. Daddy King gathered his family together and told them that Martin's vision would die along with him unless they all forgave the murderer. Together the family wept and grieved and prayed until they could forgive. The family left once more united in their commitment to non-violence. They have carried this so far that Martin Luther King, Jr.'s son appealed for a new trial for James Earl Ray, who was convicted of Martin's murder, several months before Ray's death.

Would the Civil Rights Movement ever have happened in the United States if Daddy King had not learned to forgive white people? It seems that the entire King family's sealed orders includes promoting racial justice through non-violence, and Daddy King was instrumental in healing the hurts that might have stood in their way.

## Acting On Our Sealed Orders Can Heal Hurts

The above story of Daddy King emphasizes the need to heal hurts before we can go on with our purpose in life. However, even in the process of healing their hurts the King family used the gift of reconciliation that was so much a part of their sealed orders. Often, beginning to live out our sealed orders in even a small way allows us to take in the life we need to heal our hurts.

For example, when Dennis and Sheila married, I (Matt) was devastated. Dennis and I had lived and worked together in the Jesuit community for twenty-seven years. After Sheila joined us, we gave all our retreats together as a team of three. I could not imagine continuing without them, yet it seemed unlikely our work together would go on. I could give a third of a retreat as part of our team, but I had no confidence that I could give a whole one alone. Most of all, I felt so hurt myself that I feared giving retreats on healing hurts in which I might be overwhelmed by my own pain.

Although I had felt quite clear for many years that writing books and giving retreats on healing were the activities that most helped me live out my sealed orders, now I wanted to cancel everything on my schedule. The retreat I most wanted to cancel was a Spanish one for a community that did not want to include Dennis and Sheila now that they were married. I didn't want to go to a place where Dennis and Sheila weren't welcome. And, since their Spanish is better than mine, I would never have accepted the invitation without them.

I called and tried to cancel, but the coordinators told me the publicity was already out and they were counting on me. When I said I couldn't give a Spanish talk alone, they assured me that I could speak in English and they would translate. I asked to come three days early so I could live with a Spanish family. I wanted time to practice my Spanish enough to at least understand it, even if I couldn't speak it.

I stayed with an elderly couple, Raul and Maria Fernandez, who could speak no English. I felt so loved by them that I relaxed and worried less about all the mistakes I was making in Spanish. When I told Raul how relieved I would be to speak English at the conference, I was shocked by his response. He said the leaders had decided they wanted me to speak in Spanish after all, because they would feel what was in my heart directly rather than through an interpreter. That mattered more to them than perfect grammar.

Frightened and insecure as I was, I felt so loved by Raul and Maria that I agreed to give my talk in Spanish. The next day, as I stood before a thousand people and spoke in broken Spanish, I was surprised by how connected I felt to them. When I finished, they applauded loudly. I received *un monton de abrazos* (a mountain of hugs) and several invitations to speak to other Spanish groups. Each hug restored my confidence that I could still live out my sealed orders by giving healing retreats without worrying whether they would be as good as before or whether I would be overwhelmed with pain. The important thing was to risk doing what I knew I had come here to do, and letting my sealed orders—my unique way of giving and receiving love—continue to heal me as it did that day. And, as it turned out, Dennis and Sheila and I have been able to continue our ministry together in even more fruitful ways than before.

Now, whenever I am hurt and feel paralyzed in my ability to carry out my sealed orders, I remember how God healed me at the Spanish retreat. I remind myself that God can set me free in the same way again. The passage from Romans 8:28 that tells us, "We know that all things work together for good for those who love God, who are called according to God's purpose," has new meaning for me. I now understand it to mean that God has a special purpose for each of us, and that God will use our hurts and mistakes to accomplish that good purpose.

## Our Greatest Fault Can Reveal Our Sealed Orders

This promise that God will use even our hurts and mistakes in the service of our sealed orders also means that our greatest fault can be a *felix culpa* (happy fault) or blessing. My greatest fault is my perfectionism. Thus, for example, I wanted to cancel the retreat because I knew that in Spanish I would make ten times more mistakes. Perfectionists like myself can't risk making mistakes.

But as I made mistakes and let myself be loved by the Spanish-speaking community, I began to receive love right into the perfectionism that I hated. I experienced healing of the hurt underlying my perfectionism, that of not feeling loved as a child when I didn't do things right. Because I felt loved unconditionally by Raul, Maria and their friends, I began to care more about sharing my heart in healing ways than about speaking perfect Spanish. My perfectionistic drive to always be right could then express itself as a loving desire to make things whole (my sealed orders), even at the risk of making mistakes. Thus my greatest fault and my sealed orders are two faces of the same coin.

Because our faults are simply ways our greatest gifts have become distorted through hurts, one clue to our sealed orders will often be what we like least about ourselves. For example, I (Dennis) have already mentioned my tendency to bend over backwards to avoid offending others. This is a distortion of the same energy that underlies my sealed orders of being a brother. What I (Sheila) like least about myself is my tendency to be overly sensitive to the needs and problems of others. However, this is the same energy that allows me to care so sensitively for creation.

As each of the three of us allows love to touch what we like least about ourselves and the underlying hurts, we have a greater awareness of and capacity to carry out our sealed orders. So, if your faults seem more obvious than your sealed orders, you can ask yourself two questions: "What do I like least about myself?" and "If I felt loved with this fault, how might I imagine myself using the same energy to give and receive love with others?" As we receive love into our faults and the hurts underlying them, we are freed to use the same energies driving our faults to carry out our sealed orders.

## ❧ HEALING PROCESS

**1.** Take a moment to grow quiet within and breathe in the love of God. Get in touch with as much as you know at this time of your sealed orders.

**2.** Recall a time when you felt deeply loved and free to carry out your special purpose in life. Breathe deeply, breathing in that love and letting it fill you again.

**3.** Now recall a time when you were hurt and felt disconnected from your own unique way of giving and receiving love. Notice any feelings related to the hurt and allow yourself to experience them.

**4.** Let yourself be loved by God in the midst of these feelings, without trying to fix or change them. It may help to return to the moment of deep love when you felt able to carry out your special purpose, and breathe that love into this hurt.

**5.** Now ask yourself if there is any way you could act on your sealed orders that would help continue to heal this hurt as you give and receive love.

## CHAPTER 8

# Sealed Orders in Scripture and Tradition

The foundational experience for a Christian is baptism. As we mentioned in Chapter 1, we believe baptism is about sealed orders. The Baptismal Rite celebrates the coming of another face of Jesus into the Christian community. We celebrate that each of us is an icon to help the Church discover the fullness of Jesus. If any one of us were not born, the whole Christian community would be missing a particular way of experiencing Jesus. Our sealed orders are simply a way of naming the unique aspect of Jesus that each of us reveals.

The baptismal symbols (e.g., water, white garment, oil for anointing, candle) along with their accompanying prayers all celebrate that another face of Jesus is born. For example, when John's godparents lit his baptismal candle, I (Dennis) read the accompanying liturgical prayer. This prayer reminds the community that the baptismal candle symbolizes not only that Jesus is the light of the world but also, as Matthew 5:14 proclaims, that our John is the light of the world. After the baptismal candle was lit, we invited the participants one by one to hold the candle while blessing John with the special way they experienced him bringing light or being a face of Jesus. In other words, they were blessing his sealed orders.

In all three gospel accounts, Jesus' baptism marks the beginning of his public life and signifies his commitment to his sealed orders. The gospels are the stories of how Jesus discovered and lived out his sealed orders which were to empower us to live in a new way—in what he called the reign of God.

Jesus was born into a world in which very few people could consciously choose what they wanted to do in life. It was a world of violence and domination in which a powerful minority controlled the lives of everyone else. The reign of God, on the other hand, was a way of living based on love, equality and sharing. Jesus' sealed orders seem to have included empowering us to live in this way.

None of us can carry out our sealed orders without the support of a community—not even Jesus. Jesus' baptism was his way of being empowered by others to carry out his sealed orders. The one who baptized Jesus, John, had something that Jesus needed. John the Baptist was a prophet who saw through the domination system of his time and who proclaimed the kind of savior his people needed. John baptized with water because water was a symbol of the exodus in which the Jewish people left slavery. So, the whole meaning of baptism for John was exactly what Jesus came to empower us to do: escape from a way of living based on violence and domination and enter a promised land of love, equality and sharing. In baptism we do for a new member of our community what John the Baptist did for Jesus: we bless that person with what he or she needs to make his or her special contribution to the reign of God, and we promise our support for the rest of our lives.

At our John Matthew's baptism, we asked our guests to get in touch with their own sealed orders as a way of knowing how they can be mentors to him. One friend, a psychotherapist, said, "I want to encourage John as he learns to carry others in his heart." Our brother-in-law, Mike, who owns several restaurants, said, "In this family *somebody* had better teach him about business!"

## Called by Name

Naming is a central element of any baptism. The presider asks the parents, "What name do you give this child?" In our culture, names are sometimes chosen according to what is currently fashionable. Other times they are chosen to honor or remember a saint or a special person. For example, John Matthew was named after Dennis' two brothers. In biblical times, however, names were chosen to express the essence of the person. As scripture scholar John McKenzie says,

> . . . the name is considered to be more than an artificial tag which distinguishes one person from another. The name has a mysterious identity with its bearer; it can be considered as a substitute for the person, as acting or receiving in his place. The name is often meaningful; it not only distinguishes the person, but is thought to tell something of the kind of person he is.

Thus, in Hebrew culture giving a name meant giving an identity that was the essence of the person. When Isaiah says, "Yahweh called me before I was born,

from my mother's womb he pronounced my name" (Is 49:1), he is saying that God gave him his essence—in our terms, his sealed orders—before he was born.

Before John the Baptist was born, the angel Gabriel announced the child's name to his father, Zechariah. John means "Yahweh has shown favor." John's sealed orders were to proclaim God's favor in sending us a savior. Before Jesus was born, the angel Gabriel announced to Mary that her son would be called Jesus, meaning "Yahweh saves." Jesus' sealed orders were to be the savior of the world.

This suggests to us that, like John the Baptist and Jesus, when God pronounced our names before we were born, God gave us our essence, our sealed orders that make us unique from everyone else on earth. In biblical times, because the name was so connected with the unique mission of the person, when God invited a person to carry out his or her mission that person sometimes received a new name from God. Thus, Abram became Abraham (meaning father of nations) and Simon became Peter (meaning rock), etc.

As parents, we (Dennis and Sheila) believe one of our primary responsibilities is to help our John find his real name. We like the summary of *The Spiritual Exercises* that we once heard from Bert Thelen, S.J. He said they are about finding our own name, the special name by which God calls us. St. Ignatius trusted that everyone was capable of finding that name. Ignatius believed this so radically that he assumed a scrubwoman doing her best to listen could hear God as clearly as a mystic who had spent years in prayer.

In Chapter 3, we referred to the examen. Ignatius begins *The Spiritual Exercises* by recommending that every person be taught the examen—implicitly including the scrubwoman. Ignatius saw the examen as so fundamental to the spiritual life that, when the Jesuits attending the Council of Trent had little time for prayer, Ignatius told them they could skip anything but the examen. According to Herbert Alphonso, the real purpose of the examen is to ask ourselves every day to what extent we are living according to the special name by which God calls us. For example, when I do the daily examen, I (Dennis) can ask myself, "When today did I most experience myself as brother?" and "When today did I least experience myself as brother?" Our "name" can give direction for each day as well as for all of life.

Perhaps when God talked with us from all eternity about our sealed orders, the conversation included something like, "By what name shall I call you?" If each of us asks himself or herself, "By what name do I hear God calling me?" Dennis hears "Brother," Matt hears "Healer," and Sheila hears "Care for Creation." When God welcomes you home, by what name will God greet you?

## ☙ HEALING PROCESS

**1.** Take a moment to grow quiet within and breathe in the love of God.

**2.** Recall a time when someone spoke your name lovingly. You may think of a parent or grandparent, a spouse, a special friend, etc. Imagine yourself with that person, and hear once again the tenderness with which he or she pronounced your name.

**3.** Now imagine yourself with God before you were born, about to be sent forth into this world after agreeing to your sealed orders. As God hands you an envelope containing your sealed orders, what name is written on it?

**4.** Say this name to yourself, repeating it as often as necessary until you can say it with the same intensity and feeling as you imagine God saying it to you. Continue to breathe deeply, breathing in God's love for you and God's blessing on your sealed orders.

# *Process for Group Sharing*

Following is a suggested format for using this book with a wide variety of groups, such as families, parish study groups, Christian Initiation groups, 12-Step recovery groups, prison inmates, youth groups, patients in group psychotherapy, etc. The course can have six sessions (one each for Chapters 3 through 8), or the length can be adjusted to suit the needs of the group. Each member of the group will need a copy of this book.

This format takes $1\frac{1}{2}$ to 2 hours for each session. Feel free to vary the format as needed. Normally groups meet once per week, but you may wish to vary the frequency of meetings. For example, you may wish to meet every two weeks or you may wish to have several sessions over one weekend.

## I.  Group Meetings

A.  Common Opening Prayer *(5 minutes)*

B.  Reading or Review of Chapter *(15 to 30 minutes)*
Beginning with Chapter 3, review this session's chapter in the book and do the healing process toward the end of the chapter. (Prior to the first session, participants may wish to read the Introduction and Chapters 1 and 2.)

C.  Silent Reflection *(3 minutes)*
Quiet time to get in touch with what part of the chapter moved your heart most deeply.

D.  Guided Journaling *(Optional—10 minutes)*
1.  Write down what is in your heart. Write as if you were writing a letter to your best friend—Jesus or God as you understand God—sharing what you feel most deeply. Don't worry about having the "right" words, but only try to share your heart. If you find it more helpful, draw a picture rather than write a letter.
2.  Now get in touch with how God is responding to you, as God speaks to you from within. You might do this by asking what is the most loving response that Jesus or God as you understand God could possibly make to you in response to what you have just shared.
3.  Write God's response. Perhaps it will be just one word or one sentence. Or perhaps it will be a simple drawing. You can be sure anything you write or draw that helps you to know more that you are loved is at least part of what God wants to say to you.

E.  Companion Sharing *(5 minutes minimum for each person to share his or her reaction to this session's material and to the home experiences during the past week.)* By the second session, each person should choose one or two companions for companion sharing and companion prayer. If possible, companions should remain together throughout the course.
1.  Share with your companion as much as you wish of what is in your heart from this session's chapter. Perhaps you will want to share what you have just written or drawn during the guided journaling.

2. Share with your companion your experience at home since you last met, especially your prayer and journaling.

3. Share with your companion what you are most grateful for now and how you need help from God.

F.  Companion Prayer *(5–10 minutes of prayer for each person)*
Pray for your companion as Jesus or God as you understand God would pray. Give thanks for whatever your companion is most grateful for and pray for whatever help your companion most wants. Then reverse roles and let your companion pray for you.

G.  Group Sharing *(Optional—15 minutes minimum)*
Share with the whole group your response to this session's material and your experience at home since you last met. Some people may wish to share from their journals.

H.  Closing Snack and Celebration
An open-ended time to enjoy one another and to continue sharing.

## II.  *Preparation at Home Between Group Meetings*

A.  Daily Healing Prayer *(10 minutes or as long as you wish)*
Each day, do the healing process toward the end of that week's chapter. For example, each day of the first week do the process toward the end of Chapter 3; each day of the second week do the process toward the end of Chapter 4; etc.

B.  Daily Journal *(10 minutes)*
1. In writing or through a drawing, share with Jesus or with God as you understand God when during this healing process or during the day your heart was deeply moved.
2. Write or draw in your journal how Jesus or God responds to what you have shared. One way to get in touch with God's response is to write or draw the most loving response you can imagine.

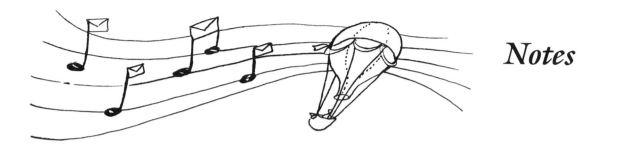

# Notes

*Pages v–vi*

Jack Kornfield, *A Path with Heart: A Guide Through the Perils and Promises of Spiritual Life* (New York: Bantam, 1993), p. 334.

## Introduction

*Page 2*

Agnes Sanford, *Sealed Orders* (Plainfield, New Jersey: Logos International, 1972).

Herbert Alphonso, S.J., *The Personal Vocation* (Rome: Centrum Ignatianum Spiritualitatis, 1992), pp. 41–43.

*Page 4*

Jean Houston, "Calling Our Spirits Home," *Noetic Sciences Review,* No. 32 (Winter, 1994), p. 9.

## Chapter 1

*Page 6*

The research on Monday as the most frequent time of death was reported by the American Heart Association (November, 1992), in *Newsweek* (December 2, 1985), p. 82, and in *U.S. News & World Report* (January 21, 1985), p. 68.

*Pages 6–7*

Study of back pain among workers at Boeing was reported by D.M. Spengler, "Back Injuries in Industry: A Retrospective Study—Overview and Cost Analysis, Injury Factors, and Employee-Related Factors," *Spine*, Vol. 11, No. 3 (1986), pp. 241–256. Cited in Larry Dossey, "Work and Health: Of Isolation, Sisyphus, and Barbarian Beds," *Alternative Therapies*, Vol. 3, No. 1 (January, 1997), pp. 8–14.

*Page 7*

See Michael Lerner, *The Politics of Meaning* (New York: Addison-Wesley, 1996). See also the journal *Tikkun*, which Rabbi Lerner edits (published by the Institute for Labor and Mental Health, 5100 Leona St., Oakland, CA 94619).

Agnes Sanford, *op. cit.*, p. 94.

*Page 8*

Joseph Chilton Pearce, *Evolution's End: Claiming the Potential of Our Intelligence* (San Francisco: Harper, 1992), pp. 189–194, and "The Roots of Intelligence" (audio tape published by Sounds True Recordings, Boulder, CO).

Bernie Siegel, *Peace, Love & Healing* (New York: Harper, 1989), p. 46.

*Pages 8–9*

Melvin Morse, *Transformed by the Light* (New York: Ivy Books, 1992), pp. 204–205 and 213.

*Pages 9–10*

William J. Young, S.J. (trans.), *St. Ignatius' Own Story* (Chicago: Loyola University Press, 1980).

*Page 10*

Herbert Alphonso, S.J., *op. cit.*, pp. 13–14.

*Page 18*

Herbert Alphonso, S.J., *op. cit.*, pp. 58–59.

Reference to Bernard Häring comes from Richard Gula, *Reason Informed by Faith: Foundations of Catholic Morality* (Mahwah, NJ: Paulist Press, 1989), pp. 78–79.

*Page 19*

Quote from David Steindl-Rast cited in Dawn Gibeau, "Caring for Your Soul at Work," *Praying*, No. 80 (Sept.-Oct., 1997), p. 12.

## Chapter 3

*Page 24*

Bernie Siegel, "How to Never Grow Old" (audio tape published by Sounds True Recordings, Boulder, CO, 1992).

*Page 25*

Dennis Linn, Sheila Fabricant Linn & Matthew Linn, *Sleeping with Bread: Holding What Gives You Life* (Mahwah, NJ: Paulist Press, 1995).

*Page 27*

Focusing was originally developed by Eugene Gendlin at the University of Chicago. See his book *Focusing* (New York: Bantam, 1978). We learned focusing from Peter Campbell and Edwin McMahon, who have integrated it with Christian spirituality, and we have built upon their method. We are indebted to Pete and Ed for the idea (paraphrased on page 37) that "Discernment is how grace feels in the body." For an excellent brief introduction to focusing, see Peter Campbell, "Focusing: Doorway to the Body-Life of Spirit," *Creation Spirituality* (May/June, 1991), 24, 26, 27, 50, 52. For a listing of books and retreats on focusing, contact: Institute for Bio-Spiritual Research, P.O. Box 741137, Arvada, CO 80006-1137.

*Pages 31–32*

Robert Coles, *A Radical Devotion* (Reading, MA: Addison-Wesley, 1987) p. xviii.

*Page 32*

Clara Hale's story was reported by NBC News, December, 1992; cited in Mark Link, *Vision 2000* (Allen, TX: Tabor, 1991), p. 96.

Quote from Frederick Buechner is found in Rich Heffern, *Adventures in Simple Living* (New York: Crossroad, 1994), p. 78.

*Pages 32–33*

Bernie Siegel, "How to Never Grow Old," *op. cit.*

*Page 36*

Herbert Alphonso, *op. cit.*, p. 30.

## Chapter 4

*Page 37*

William R. Miller, "Spirituality and Addictions," address presented at "Spirituality in Health Care Conference," Albuquerque, New Mexico, April, 1997. See also William R. Miller, R. Gayle Benefield, and J. Scott Tonigan, "Enhancing Motivation for Change in Problem Drinking: A Controlled Comparison of Two Therapist Styles," *Journal of Consulting And Clinical Psychology*, Vol. 61, No. 3 (1993), pp. 455-461.

*Page 39*

Melvin Morse, *Transformed by the Light, op. cit.*, pp. 163-165.

Dr. Bruce Greyson's research was reported in Dr. Raymond Moody and Dr. Melvin Morse, "Near Death Experiences" (audio tape published by Sounds True Recordings, Boulder, CO, 1991).

*Page 41*

For an account of Newman's near-fatal illness, see Charles Healey, S.J., *Modern Spiritual Writers* (New York: Alba House, 1988), pp. 174-184.

Newman's meditation is from John Henry Newman, *Meditations and Devotions* (Westminster, MD: Christian Classics, 1975), p. 301.

The physiological healing effects on the brain of near-death experiences are reported in Morse, *op. cit.*, pp. 158-159.

*Page 43*

The poem "God Says Yes to Me" by Kaylin Haught is from *In the Palm of Your Hand* by Steve Kowit (Gardiner, ME: Tilbury House, 1995) and is used with the author's permission.

## Chapter 5

*Page 47*

Quote regarding Aquinas' love of created things is from G.K. Chesterton, *Saint Thomas Aquinas* (Garden City, NY: Image, 1956), p. 119.

## Chapter 6

*Page 52*

Dr. Benjamin Spock, *Baby and Child Care* (New York: Pocket Books, 1985), p. 79. Cited in Jane Hirschmann, "Raising Children Free of Food and Weight Problems," *Mothering* (Summer, 1989), pp. 27-31. In addition to warning about the damaging effects of artificial foods such as sugar on a baby's innate ability to choose wholesome foods, Aletha Solter emphasizes that babies can be trusted to choose a balanced diet "only if the babies have not been interfered with in any way. If they have been undernursed, over-nursed, or coaxed, tricked, or forced to eat certain foods, then they may have lost the ability to know what their bodies need." See her book, *The Aware Baby* (Goleta, CA: Shining Star Press, 1984), pp. 114-120, 124.

On eating as remembering, see Brian Swimme, *The Universe Is a Green Dragon* (Santa Fe, NM: Bear & Co, 1985), pp. 105-106.

On exercise, see Swimme, *op. cit.*, p. 106.

*Page 54*

James Hillman, *The Soul's Code* (New York: Random House, 1996), p. 89.

Catherine Sneed shares her story in Carol Olwell (ed.), *Gardening from the Heart* (Berkeley, CA: Antelope Island Press, 1990), pp. 155-162.

Hillman, *op. cit.*, p. 75.

*Pages 54–55*

For Aquinas' attitude toward nature, see Chesterton, *op. cit.*, Chapters 3 and 4.

*Page 55*

For a discussion of the meaning of *doxa* and the quote from David Bohm, see Matthew Fox, "Exploring the Cosmic Christ Archetype," audio tape published by Friends of Creation Spirituality, Oakland, CA.

For Ignatius' emphasis upon finding the presence of God in all things, see Louis J. Puhl (ed.), *The Spiritual Exercises of St. Ignatius* (Chicago: Loyola University Press, 1951), No. 39, pp. 235 and 236.

*Page 58*

The idea that we are the rainforest, etc. become conscious of itself has been suggested by several prominent figures in ecology, such as Joanna Macy in "Working for the Earth Without Going Crazy," *Radical Grace*, Vol. 6, No. 1 (February-March, 1993). This seems to us another way of expressing Teilhard de Chardin's vision of the whole earth emerging into consciousness, as expressed in *The Phenomenon of Man* (New York: Harper & Row, 1961).

Hillman, *op. cit.*, p. 87.

*Pages 59–60*

Archbishop Hunthausen's story is quoted in Kathleen Fischer & Thomas Hart, *Facing Discouragement* (Mahwah, NJ: Paulist Press, 1997), p. 53.

## Chapter 7

*Pages 61–63*

The story of Daddy King was reported in a BBC documentary.

## Chapter 8

*Page 68*

John L. McKenzie, S.J., *Dictionary of the Bible* (New York: Macmillan, 1965), p. 603.

*Page 70*

Bert Thelen's comment was made during a talk given at the Jesuit Reunion held at Marquette University in July, 1991.

Since God's will or special name for each of us is so essential, God wants to reveal this to every person. The mystic may have more time and tools than the scrubwoman to listen to God, but God asks a person to do only the best he or she can do. See Jules Toner, S.J., *Discerning God's Will* (St. Louis: Institute of Jesuit Sources, 1991), pp. 312–315.

Herbert Alphonso, S.J., *op. cit.*, pp. 64 and 83-91.

# Resources for Further Growth
# by the Authors

## Books

*Simple Ways to Pray for Healing* (1998). This book contains the eight simple ways of praying for healing that we have returned to most often in our ministry, and integrates spirituality with contemporary physics and psychology. These ways of praying are simple enough for small children, yet profound enough to touch sophisticated adults.

*Don't Forgive Too Soon: Extending the Two Hands That Heal* (1997). When we are hurt, we are tempted to either act as a passive doormat or to strike back and escalate the cycle of violence. We can avoid both of these temptations and find creative responses to hurts by moving through the five stages of forgiveness. In so doing, we discover the two hands of non-violence: one hand that stops the person who hurt us and the other that reaches out, calms that person and offers new life. This book has healing processes so simple that children can use them.

*Sleeping with Bread: Holding What Gives You Life* (1995). A simple process—for individuals and for families and others to share—of reflecting on each day's consolation and desolation. This process can help us get in touch each day with both hurts and healing, guide our decisions and help us find the purpose of our life. Includes a question and answer section at the end. Especially recommended for family spirituality.

*Good Goats: Healing Our Image of God* (1994). We become like the God we adore. Thus, one of the easiest ways to heal ourselves and our society is to heal our image of God, so that we know a God who loves us at least as much as those who love us the most. Discusses whether God throws us into hell or otherwise vengefully punishes us, and the role of free will. Includes a question and answer section that gives the theological and scriptural foundation for the main text.

*Healing Spiritual Abuse & Religious Addiction* (1994). Why does religion help some people grow in wholeness, yet seem to make others become more rigid and stuck? Discusses religious addiction and spiritual abuse, and offers ways of healing the shame-based roots of these behaviors. Includes how spiritual abuse can also be sexually abusive, and how scripture has often been used to reinforce religious addiction and spiritual abuse. Concludes with an image of healthy religion, in which we are free to do what Jesus would do.

*Belonging: Bonds of Healing & Recovery* (1993). 12-Step recovery from any compulsive pattern is integrated with contemporary spirituality and psychology. This book helps the reader discover the genius underneath every addiction. Defines addiction as rooted in abuse and as our best attempt to belong to ourselves, others, God and the universe. Recovery comes from finding a better way to belong.

*Healing the Eight Stages of Life* (1988). Based on Erik Erikson's developmental system, this book helps to heal hurts and develop gifts at each stage of life, from conception through old age. Includes healing ways our image of God has been formed and deformed at each stage.

*Healing the Greatest Hurt* (1985). Healing the deepest hurt most people experience, the loss of a loved one, by learning to give and receive love with the deceased through the Communion of Saints.

*Praying with Another for Healing* (1984). Guide to praying with another to heal hurts such as sexual abuse, depression, loss of a loved one, etc.

*To Heal as Jesus Healed* (with Barbara Shlemon Ryan; 1978, revised 1997). This book, also on praying with another, emphasizes physical healing, including the healing power of the Sacrament of the Sick.

*Healing the Dying* (with Mary Jane Linn; 1979). How the seven last words of Jesus can help us prepare for death . . . and also for life.

*Healing Life's Hurts: Healing Memories through the Five Stages of Forgiveness* (1978, revised 1993). Contains a thorough discussion of the five stages of dying and how they apply to the process of forgiveness. This is our most complete resource on forgiveness.

*Healing of Memories* (1974). A simple guide to inviting Jesus into our painful memories to help us forgive ourselves and others.

These and other books by the authors (except *To Heal As Jesus Healed*) are available from Paulist Press, 997 Macarthur Blvd., Mahwah, NJ 07430, Phone orders (800) 218-1903, FAX orders (800) 836-3161. *To Heal As Jesus Healed* is available from Resurrection Press, P.O. Box 248, Williston Park, NY 11596, Phone (516) 742-5686, FAX (516) 746-6872.

## *Tapes & Courses* (for use alone, with a companion, or with a group)

*Simple Ways to Pray for Healing* (1998). Audio or videotapes to accompany book.

*Good Goats: Healing Our Image of God* (1994). Two-part videotape to accompany book (see above).

*Healing Our Image of God* (1994). Set of two audio tapes that may be used to accompany the book *Good Goats: Healing Our Image of God* and/or *Healing Spiritual Abuse & Religious Addiction*.

*Healing Spiritual Abuse & Religious Addiction* (1994). Audio tapes to accompany book (see above).

*Belonging: Healing & 12 Step Recovery* (1992). Audio or videotapes and a course guide to accompany book (see above), for use as a program of recovery.

*Healing the Eight Stages of Life* (1991). Tapes and a course guide that can be used with book (see above) as a course in healing the life cycle. Available in video and audio versions.

*Prayer Course for Healing Life's Hurts* (1983). Ways to pray for personal healing that integrate physical, emotional, spiritual and social dimensions. Book includes course guide, and tapes are available in video and audio versions.

*Praying with Another for Healing* (1984). Tapes that can be used with book (see above). Book includes course guide, and tapes are available in video and audio versions. *Healing the Greatest Hurt* (see above) may be used as supplementary reading for the last five of these sessions, which focus on healing of grief for the loss of a loved one.

*Dying to Live: Healing through Jesus' Seven Last Words* (with Bill & Jean Carr, 1983). How the seven last words of Jesus empower us to fully live the rest of our life. Tapes (available in video or audio versions) may be used with the book *Healing the Dying* (with Mary Jane Linn, 1979).

Audio tapes for all of these courses are available from Christian Video Library, 3914-A Michigan Ave., St. Louis, MO 63118, phone (314) 865-0729, FAX (314) 773-3115.

Videotapes for all of these courses (except *Good Goats*) are also available from Christian Video Library. *Good Goats* may be purchased from Paulist Press, 997 Macarthur Boulevard, Mahwah, NJ 07430, phone (800) 218-1903 or (201) 825-7300, FAX (800) 836-3161.

## Videotapes on a Donation Basis

To borrow any of the above videotapes, contact Christian Video Library (address and telephone above).

## Spanish Books & Tapes

Several of the above books and tapes are available in Spanish. For information, contact Christian Video Library.

## Retreats & Conferences

For retreats and conferences by the authors on the material in this book and on other topics in the resources listed above, contact Dennis, Sheila & Matthew Linn, c/o Re-Member Ministries, 3914-A Michigan Ave., St. Louis, MO 63118, Phone (970) 476-9235 or (314) 865-0729, FAX (970) 476-9235 or (314) 773-3115.

## About the Authors

Dennis, Sheila and Matt Linn work together as a team, integrating physical, emotional and spiritual wholeness, having worked as hospital chaplains and therapists, and currently in leading retreats and spiritual companioning. They have taught courses on processes for healing in over forty countries and in many universities and hospitals, including a course to doctors accredited by the American Medical Association. Dennis and Matt are the co-authors of sixteen books, the last eleven co-authored with Sheila. These books have sold over a million copies in English and have been translated into more than fifteen different languages. Dennis and Sheila live in Colorado with their son, John, and Matt lives in a Jesuit community in Minnesota.

## About the Illustrator

Francisco Miranda lives in Mexico City. In addition to illustrating *Good Goats: Healing Our Image of God, Healing Spiritual Abuse & Religious Addiction, Sleeping with Bread: Holding What Gives You Life,* and *Don't Forgive Too Soon: Extending the Two Hands That Heal,* he has also written and illustrated several children's books. He is a renowned artist and sculptor, whose work has been widely exhibited.